A Wildflower Thrives in Florida

A Wildflower Thrives in Florida

From Striving to Thriving
after Sexual Abuse and Other Trauma

Julie Woodley
Foreword by H. Norman Wright

RESOURCE *Publications* · Eugene, Oregon

A WILDFLOWER THRIVES IN FLORIDA
From Striving to Thriving after Sexual Abuse and Other Trauma

Copyright © 2019 Julie Woodley. All rights reserved. Except for brief quotations in critical publications or reviews, no part of this book may be reproduced in any manner without prior written permission from the publisher. Write: Permissions, Wipf and Stock Publishers, 199 W. 8th Ave., Suite 3, Eugene, OR 97401.

Resource Publications
An Imprint of Wipf and Stock Publishers
199 W. 8th Ave., Suite 3
Eugene, OR 97401

www.wipfandstock.com

PAPERBACK ISBN: 978-1-5326-7276-7
HARDCOVER ISBN: 978-1-5326-7277-4
EBOOK ISBN: 978-1-5326-7278-1

Manufactured in the U.S.A.   APRIL 2, 2019

Scripture references taken from the following sources:

THE HOLY BIBLE, NEW INTERNATIONAL VERSION®, NIV® Copyright © 1973, 1978, 1984, 2011 by Biblica, Inc.™ Used by permission. All rights reserved worldwide.

The Holy Bible, New King James Version®. Copyright © 1982 by Thomas Nelson, Inc. All rights reserved.

Scripture quotations marked (NLT) are taken from the Holy Bible, New Living Translation, copyright © 1996, 2004, 2007 by Tyndale House Foundation. Used by permission of Tyndale House Publishers, Inc., Carol Stream, Illinois 60188. All rights reserved.

Scripture quotations from *THE MESSAGE*. Copyright © by Eugene H. Peterson 1993, 1994, 1995, 1996, 2000, 2001, 2002. Used by permission of NavPress Publishing Group.

Scripture quotations taken from the New American Standard Bible®, Copyright © 1960, 1962, 1963, 1968, 1971, 1972, 1973, 1975, 1977, 1995 by The Lockman Foundation. Used by permission. (www.Lockman.org)

Dedicated to all the women who feel they have no hope: dare to hope again. I pray God turns your tears and trauma into great desire and dreams—you are loved far more than you can ever imagine!

Contents

Foreword by H. Norman Wright ix
Acknowledgments xi
Introduction xiii

Chapter 1	Negative Messages	1
Chapter 2	Escape . . . No Escape	7
Chapter 3	My Constant Companion	11
Chapter 4	"Julie, I Love You"	16
Chapter 5	Something Amazing	21
Chapter 6	Old Reactions, New Reactions	27
Chapter 7	Untangling the Past	33
Chapter 8	Moving Experience	42
Chapter 9	Higher and Deeper	49
Chapter 10	Raining and Pouring	55
Chapter 11	Bridges to Healing	62
Chapter 12	Breaking Out	69
Chapter 13	Crushed but Not Destroyed	77
Chapter 14	A (Birthday) Candle in the Dark	82
Chapter 15	Embracing Trauma Far Away	87
Chapter 16	Interrupted but Restored	90

Chapter 17   A Wildflower Continues Her Adventures   95

Chapter 18   A Miracle Unfolds   118

Chapter 19   Fixing My Eyes on Jesus   124

Chapter 20   Why Do I Do This?   127

Epilogue   A Wildflower Moves to Chicago   129
Bibliography   133
About the Author   134

Foreword

Julie Woodley's story is one of healing and redemption. She is an exemplary person of integrity who consistently demonstrates mature fruit of the Holy Spirit and faithful Christian Character in all she is and in all she does. Julie possesses one of the most phenomenal testimonies of Christian redemption one will ever hear about and strives to continuously live out that transformational miracle in her relationships both personally and professionally.

She has passed some of the most difficult and painful tests life has to offer with flying colors. Consequently, Julie has been determined to glorify God in both her personal and professional life. Her ministry to hurting people has been one which I have watched through the years with admiration and support. Her heart of compassion for the hurting, insight for their painful dynamics and hope for their hearts to be healed is most impressive, refreshing and therapeutic.

Julie excels in clinical, facilitating small groups as well as her many capable gifts and talents. She serves both the traumatized as well as the average broken person with distinction, humility and grace.

Through the pain and trauma which would overwhelm any of us, God has seen fit to use healing and recovery to multitudes. Through her pain God has reached out to bring hope to so many. Her story needs to be told again and again as she draws others to the healing presence of Jesus.

Dr. H. Norman Wright

Acknowledgments

My biggest thanks go to Jesus, who entered my darkness and showed me the way into his light and love. I have no words for the gratitude I feel for you and the love I have for you. You are the knight in shining armor I always hoped to find but you were the one that found me. You are the reason my story has a joyous ending filled with extravagant hope and love! Thank you, thank you, thank you. I am overwhelmed with love and joyful anticipation for today and tomorrow!

I want to say thanks to my children: Bonnie Joy, Mathew, Jon-Michael and Wesley. I love you so much and thank God for your love in my life. Each of you has shown me something new about myself and about God's provision and care. You're such unique, gifted individuals and the Lord has blessed me very much to allow me to be your mom. Thanks for your support and encouragement as I've worked on this book.

I must say thanks to my dear friends Wayne and Norma Pederson, Jim and Sharon Goding, Anne and Rudy Migliore, Jeannette and Stan Bakke, Jeanette and Ron Vought, John Eldredge, Dr. H. Norman Wright, my grandmother and Darryl Bengston (who are still in my heart as they enjoy heaven), Willis and Kay Finifrock, Morgan and Cherie Snyder, Christopher West, Glenn Repple, and Paul Sirmons. There are so many who have loved me so well with the love of God, I could not name them all. You gave me your love and were a beacon showing me the way to the Father's love. You've been towers of strength for me and role models of what Christians should be. You've always been supportive of my story finding its way into print.

And thank you Wildflowers all over the country and now in other countries. The miracles God is doing through the In The Wildflowers and Into My Arms curriculum inspire me to continue

Acknowledgments

to live life and share the love of God wide open as I continue to heal and be restored as you are. I am so very proud of you all for your courageous healing with God; I love you all!

Thanks to my editor Clem Boyd, who helped me sort out the best way to tell my story. But most of all Clem, thank you for understanding me and helping the readers see the heart of God in me and for them! Not an easy task but one you have done so well!

Introduction

I'VE HEARD HUNDREDS AND hundreds of stories of trauma as a certified trauma counselor. Victims of all sorts of trauma come to me with their pain and shame, anger and confusion. I've listened as beautiful, precious women have told me about years of abuse at the hands of people they should have been able to trust. Their stories are heartbreaking to hear but these brave, courageous women inspire me as they voice the unvoiceable and speak the unspeakable. It puts a fire in me to keep telling my own story.

It's that same fire that has led me to tell my tale and share it with you here. My story is a story of abuse, at the hands of the man who I thought was my father. But he wasn't the only one. Others took advantage of me too. I was also my own worst enemy, living a life full of drinking, parties and sex, but never being satisfied or discovering anything that would fill up that love vacuum in my heart. I was soooo completely empty.

My goal in telling my story is not to make you love me, feel sorry for me or even understand me. My great desire is to be a healer who heals, and so, I give you my own shattered life on paper, my search for love, and the answer that came to me out of the blackness of a planned suicide. My recovery is a miracle and God has given me the remarkable gift of letting me speak to many, many others about the wholeness and tenderness that is ours through Jesus.

The Apostle Paul told his story of being a violent, hateful man, not for anything he could gain, but to let others know that even though he was "the worst of sinners" Jesus Christ came into the world to save people like him. Paul's story is still an amazing example to others thirsting for acceptance and restoration. If Jesus could rescue a man like Paul then there's hope for anyone "who would believe on him and receive eternal life." (1 Timothy 1:15–16,

Introduction

NIV). I desire, in some small way, to follow Paul's example in the coming pages.

I have had a number of coaches, counselors and confidants on this journey. The path to having a life bursting forth with the goodness God intends requires finding trustworthy traveling companions. I would advise anyone reading my story to begin praying, right this second, about who they might meet with, a sex abuse or trauma recovery group they might join, a therapist or counselor they could begin seeing. This is no time for pulling yourself up by your own bootstraps. I've tried it and nearly made myself crazy with grief.

You have to push against that feeling inside that makes you want to shut out everyone from your pain. Most of the time you'll want to run from the hurt. That's why you need someone who will hold your hand and be with you through it. The way to healing is with others, not without them. You've done that for far too long, trying to handle your sadness, shame and loss all by yourself. Promise me right now you'll get on the internet or talk to someone in your church or search in a phone book to locate someone or some group that will walk with you on the long hike to completeness. Better yet, promise yourself you won't try to do this alone.

There are moments, even with gifted, compassionate helpers, that you may still feel alone. And that's where Jesus meets me. That's where he enters my trauma and shows me his hands and feet. My Lord and savior was abused and he has the scars, for all eternity, to prove it. He wants to be there for you too, in the middle of your messy emotions, and to release you from your shame and self-hate. He can give you strength to forgive yourself and others. If you don't know Him, introduce yourself to Him and let Him begin to love you and save your life.

Chapter 1

Negative Messages

Confused and Ashamed

I'VE ALWAYS LOVED THE rugged beauty of the Rockies. When most children were learning to ride their bicycles, I would saddle up my gentle horse Chico and together we'd wander on the desolate mountain trails. After memorizing nearly every turn on those silent trails, Chico and I became like best friends.

Chico would lift me up so I could pick wild apples and then, with his huge teeth, he'd pick one for himself. On summer mornings he and I would follow the wild, winding trails along the Kootenai River until we found a valley of wildflowers. Exhausted and happy we would sleep away the hot afternoons.

In a way Chico was not only my traveling companion he was also my protector. To many people in our quiet logging town, it might sound strange that I needed a protector. After all, my father was a wealthy and respectable man. He was a successful businessman, an active church member and an industrious volunteer. He looked like the perfect protector.

Unfortunately, my father also carried a deep rage in his soul, a rage that lay hidden until he came home at night and the storms would begin. Behind the walls of that peaceful log home, my daddy's fury would rain down. I spent many days and hours terrified.

The worst of all

The abuse started before kindergarten. There was a constant barrage of soul-wounding, shame-filled messages: "You're so stupid; you'll never amount to anything; can't you do anything right?" These statements confused me because I hadn't done anything to deserve them. "I must be a bad person," I told myself. I felt worthless and began to believe the words my father would tell me every day: stupid, no good, ugly. These feelings of worthlessness intensified later with physical abuse.

Finally and most damaging of all, my father began to sexually abuse me when I was about 6 years old. When my mother was away, he would touch me in ways that filled me with shame and confusion. He told me that all fathers and daughters did this. He taught me what to do to please him sexually. "It will feel good for you too," he assured me. At the same time, he told me I must never share this "secret" with anybody.

Why did he tell me not to tell anyone about what we were doing? Why did this thing we were doing feel so icky and good at the same time? I was so confused because it was the only time he ever showed me any affection or hugged me or said he loved me. And it always had to be our secret; I was never allowed to tell anyone. And he warned me if I told anyone he would kill me. I knew he was serious.

My brother developed pretty severe sexual addictions from a very young age. So after teaching me how to satisfy him, my father encouraged me to make my brother happy. "Go ahead, I'll give you a special treat," my dad would whisper. My brother would come into my bedroom at night and I had to make him happy too. That was my job, to bring sunshine to him and others.

I'm sickened and saddened now as I realize how twisted and perverse my father's counsel was. It's like opening a box full of pain that I've kept in a deep recess in my mind. But I didn't know any better then. When you're little you trust your father without question. But I was the victim of sexual abuse.

I didn't have anyone to talk to about what was happening. I hoped against hope that my mother might be a source of refuge in this storm, but she was just another dark cloud, hurting me with comments like "You're stupid" and "You're so ugly." I had nowhere to turn. I knew I couldn't let any of the secrets out about my father so I kept it all in and thought it was just a normal thing. I felt I was a bad person, I was no good and I was alive just to satisfy men's sexual desires.

So I locked up this shameful secret, making it a prisoner in the dungeon of my wounded heart. I knew terrible things would happen if I ever unlocked and freed this awful truth.

The power of a secret

The "secret" and my father's turbulent anger held me in a tight grip of terror. When talking with teachers or neighbors, my eyes always wandered or focused on my feet: someone might glimpse the "secret" in my eyes. Christian psychologist Jason Li calls this the "broken gaze." "You can't look anybody in the eyes because if you did they would be able to look into your soul and see your real condition," he says. "For many people this all begins with that mother and father relationship."[1]

Filled with shame, I vowed to be a good girl, a perfect girl. *If only I can be perfect,* I thought, *then maybe I won't get hit. Maybe my mom will notice me. Maybe my daddy won't touch me and confuse me.* Like a terrified rabbit, I would dart from one project to the next—baking cookies, stacking wood, fixing fences—desperately trying to please dad and mom. But then I would burn the cookies or stack the wood too slow and the abuse would start again.

Profiting at my expense

It wasn't enough that my father began abusing me, and permitted my brother to do the same, but then he profited from me. I wouldn't have known what sexual trafficking was back then, but I know now I was a victim of it. My father fattened his wallet by selling me to others.

I can still remember our neighbor George handing money to my father, then taking me by the hand and walking to his house. I was 9 and 10 years old. His wife Jane was never around. As I got older, about 12 or 13, I was able to babysit. I would go to George's house and see pictures drawn on the chalkboard and dirty words. I knew they were for me; the kids were too young to read. But they could see the pictures and I would quickly erase them away. George always came home alone, after the kids were asleep, and do to me what the pictures portrayed. "Please, Jane, come home," I would plead in my mind. "Please, someone erase the pictures in my head."

My father always promised I would get the babysitting money but I never saw it, except when George gave it to him. I was just directed to make my neighbor happy. Later George was accused of sexually abusing other little girls. My parents were disgusted that girls would make up such lies. "They probably seduced him," they would say. "He's the banker; such a nice guy."

When I was 16 I was sent away for the summer to visit my Uncle Dave and his family. I had never been away from home. The last words from my father were those fateful, loathsome words, "Make your Uncle Dave happy now." Why did everyone else's happiness make me feel so miserable and filthy?

Uncle Dave and my aunt had separate bedrooms and I was advised to sleep on a couch outside his. One night he led me into his bedroom and I was so freaked out. There were big posters of naked women, all with red hair. At that time I had long red hair; I got a lump in my throat and started to shake. Uncle Dave was handicapped from a motorcycle accident. "Feel sorry for Uncle Dave," my father's words echoed in my mind. "You'll bring him happiness." How perverted to play on my sympathetic nature to encourage something so evil.

What a nightmare of a summer as I helped Uncle Dave with his red-headed obsession. I worked hard on his farm that summer but never saw a penny. I was treated like a slave in the bedroom and out.

That fall my father arranged for me to work in a hotel making men "happy" on Friday nights. The hotel was dark, depressing, and smelled bad. It had all the ambience of a garbage bin on trash day. I was so afraid, but my father assured me I was going there to babysit. I never saw any children, only men groping at me. My job was to sell drinks and go with them if they wanted me. I was only 16 but my father warned, "Don't you dare tell anyone how old you are."

I was allowed to keep bar tips but I could see the hotel manager exchanging money with my father when he picked me up. "I'm so proud of you for making those men happy," he said on the way home. It was the only time he ever said he was proud of me, but I felt dirty, used up, and discarded like a piece of tissue. "Someone take me away from all of this," I screamed in my head. "But I've got to keep smiling and making men happy." I hated Fridays. I wanted to be normal and have a normal job. Normal was a distant, unreachable dream.

Your Time:

- Briefly write or depict your story of trauma in a journal or using some other medium. Please use any vehicle that works best for you, such as narrative, poetry, music, drawings, drama, video, etc. Talk with God as you work through your story.

- In what ways did your family keep sexual abuse a secret? In what ways have you brought your trauma into the light? Try to say just one word to God right now that might help you bring your tragedy into the open. Maybe it's a word like "hurt" or "pain" or "father" or "mom". Just begin with one word.

- What is power? What does it mean to be a powerful person? Who in your life was or is powerful?

- The following is a description of Jesus by the prophet Isaiah. Read these words slowly, taking a deep breath after each period. Let these words flow over you and through you. Yelling and shouting are not power. Putting out what little fire is left in a person isn't power. With gentleness, steadfastness and tenderness God brings what's right into our lives and into the world:

A Wildflower Thrives in Florida

> He will not shout or cry out,
> or raise his voice in the streets.
> A bruised reed he will not break,
> and a smoldering wick he will not snuff out.
> In faithfulness he will bring forth justice;
> he will not falter or be discouraged
> till he establishes justice on earth. (Isaiah 42:2-4, NIV)

Chapter 2

Escape . . . No Escape

Numbing the Pain

Since I couldn't escape the pain in my home or in my heart I quickly learned to numb it. The drug of choice during my teenage years was pot. I smoked a lot of it with my boyfriend Brian. I didn't really like the feeling after I smoked it but I desperately wanted to fit in somewhere. I also drank a lot. Alcohol and marijuana were the quickest and cheapest ways to medicate my hurting soul. They helped me forget the painful memories, the cutting words, the constant fear and the rough hands of my father.

There was something even more "magical" than alcohol or marijuana—sex. I used sexual activity to medicate the pain, heal my loneliness and escape the turmoil in my home. Of course, I wasn't really looking for sex. More than anything, my little girl's heart yearned for my father's safe embrace. I longed for something pure, straight and true. Daddies should always love their little girls but instead my father communicated a twisted, confusing lesson: love equals sex. So with an addictive hunger, I gave myself to men in an attempt to find real love.

One of those men was my boyfriend Brian. I desperately wanted Brian to love me so we began to have sex often, sometimes 2 to 3 times a day. I would write in my diary when we were intimate. If I did what he wanted he would love me, right?

I also slept with other guys that would have me, putting a star in my diary every time I had sex. Sometimes I would place a couple stars on one day because the neighbor boys would gang up on me and take advantage of me. I was very, very vulnerable.

Pregnant

It should come as no surprise that I became pregnant, although I didn't know it at first. Even at 17 I knew nothing about the rhythms of the female body, let alone pregnancy. I just knew the smell of food made me vomit. So I went to our small town clinic for flu-like symptoms but discovered I wasn't carrying a germ, I was carrying a baby.

News spreads fast in a small town (not to mention my aunt worked in the clinic). By the time I got home my parents already knew. They were horrified what the neighbors might think so they shut me in my room and took the phone off the hook until they could schedule an appointment at the nearest "women's clinic." For two weeks I sat in the house, alone and confused about my body, my baby and my mother and father's solution to this dilemma.

After the two weeks were up, we drove in a deep silence 260 miles to Spokane, Washington to "terminate" the pregnancy. Abortions still seemed scary and even deviant in 1975 but everyone knew they were legal. The procedure was painful and bloody. I just wanted someone to comfort me. After the abortion I got into the truck and we rode home in an empty quietness for five long hours. My parents' mission was accomplished; I knew I'd committed the unpardonable sin.

The beginning of goodbye

My father was very angry with me for becoming pregnant so he took it out on me in every way. The next year and a half was filled with violence. On one occasion he flew into a rage because I tried to go on my senior class trip without his permission.

Escape . . . No Escape

The night before the trip I slipped out of my room to sleep over at my friend Coretta's house. Dad tracked me down, walked into my girlfriend's kitchen, shoved me out to his pickup truck, knocked my head against the truck door and pushed me inside. At home he grabbed my hair and started slamming my head against the living room wall. As I started to black out, I faintly remember my mother calmly commenting, "For goodness' sake Fred, don't kill her."

When I woke later that night my whole body throbbed with pain. And then, with my head still in a daze, my dad barged into my room with a shotgun, threatening to shoot me. I knew then I had only two choices: leave or die, emotionally and possibly physically.

I waited two hours till everyone was asleep then I climbed out of my bedroom window and ran down the mountain wearing only pajamas. It was spring run-off time so the dirt trails were muddy and water was running in little streams all over. I wasn't wearing boots, so I slipped now and then and got covered with brown splatters, but I made it to my friend Julie's house. Julie's dad would not allow my father to barge into his home and take me away, not without a fight. He was a protector and he took it upon himself to guard me during those last few months of high school. My father didn't want to risk a confrontation so he stayed away. Even still, I didn't sleep very well because I was afraid my father might find me and kill me.

Graduation day finally arrived but for me it was something far different than the "Pomp and Circumstance" celebration my classmates experienced. I was going to close a door on a tragic and confusing chapter in my life.

The day after graduation I woke at 4 a.m., walked to the train station and prepared to leave my beautiful mountain town. I had saved enough money for a one-way ticket. I boarded a train with one change of clothes and no money. I couldn't risk saying goodbye to anyone or my parents would find out. I rode the train out of the mountains, crying off and on all the way to Wisconsin, where my grandparents lived.

A Wildflower Thrives in Florida

I knew I had to go but leaving home still filled me with a deep sadness. As I sat on the train fighting back tears I remembered my grandmother's huckleberry pies, the cozy bed in "Julie's room," her warm and soft lap. I remembered the family potlucks each week with my extended family where my uncles would recount their wild tales. I remembered the majestic Rockies, meadows of wildflowers and my horse Chico. These were the sweet things I left behind in the midst of the distasteful and horrible. Letting them go nearly broke my heart.

Your Time:

- How have you "survived" your trauma so far? I'll offer three options and you pick the one you've used the most and the one you've used the least, leaving a middle option uncircled:

    Alcohol/drugs—most or least
    Denial and lots of activity—most or least
    Sex—most or least

- What do you think about these strategies?
- What things do you struggle with from the abuse? Depression, anxiety, parenting, post-traumatic stress disorder, obsessive-compulsive disorders, split out, disassociation?

    Consider Matthew 11:28-29:
    > Come to me, all you who are weary and burdened, and I will give you rest. Take my yoke upon you and learn from me, for I am gentle and humble in heart, and you will find rest for your souls. (NIV)

- Have these coping behaviors ever left you weary and burdened? Have you ever experienced the "rest" Jesus offers? Maybe you're not sure if Jesus could help. Express those doubts to him and, if you're ready, ask him to show you how He can give you true and lasting rest from your trauma.

Chapter 3

My Constant Companion

Baggage

With my little suitcase I headed straight for a small town in Wisconsin, the home of my father's parents. It was the only other town I knew and as far as I was concerned, my only chance at a new beginning.

Unfortunately, I brought more baggage than just my little suitcase. The new surroundings didn't heal my broken heart, the memories of abuse or my deep spiritual emptiness. I had packed all that in my soul and took it everywhere I went. My multiple addictions to alcohol, marijuana and sex followed me to Wisconsin too.

While in Wisconsin I met Cathy, my best friend during those bewildering days. With reckless abandon we partied and drank and slept with a new guy every weekend. Every once in a while, in a quiet moment between the parties and the sex, Cathy would grab me by the shoulders, look deep into my eyes and whisper to me in a desperate and sincere way, "Julie, I'm looking for something. I don't know what it is or where it is or who it is, but I'm searching. Will you look with me?"

One thing for sure, what I was seeking I wouldn't find at my grandparents' home. The only thing I discovered there were just more wounding words. So I was on the move again. Thinking I could outdistance my past I kept running with all my might. I moved 25 times in 5 years. But the pain of my childhood and the hurt in my soul kept pace step for step. I drank and did lots of drugs. I also slept with many, many men.

A better relationship?

In the middle of my running I met John, who was kind and very handsome. His parents were well known in the little community where I had settled down. He had seven sisters and a brother; they treated me like part of the family. I loved his family. For the first time in my life I felt wanted. We dated 5 years.

John was a good man but also quite confused. We did drugs and drank a lot. We also had a lot of sex and I became pregnant with his baby. He took me to Minneapolis to abort our little one. I loved him so much and wanted to have his child. But he was on his way to law school and a great career; he didn't have time for a wife and child. I just wanted to run away and hide. But to keep John I knew I had to go through with it.

I had the abortion, even though it was very painful in every way. I went back to Wisconsin with John but our relationship hit the skids. John said I wasn't sophisticated enough for him. He was going to be a famous lawyer and needed a wife who was more refined. I was alone again and felt like trash.

Eulogy for Elizabeth

I wrote a poem about that abortion and about the daughter I never got to hold or care for. I'd like to share it with you now:

> I was never born
>
> Ten thousand days ago, ten thousand days later
>
> my Mommy wanted to keep me, she was excited to see the bump of her tummy grow as I grew

My Constant Companion

Daddy said I couldn't be born, too much trouble; He had goals, dreams. He was studying to be a lawyer-I didn't fit

we got in the car; Daddy was quiet-all he said was "if you want to stay in this relationship you must get rid of this problem"

Mommy rode the 90 miles to Minneapolis crying, she couldn't stop, she was queasy from my growing-we stopped and she threw up. "Maybe he will take me home, let me keep the baby," she hoped, she prayed. "Please turn around!"

The air was turning Spring, it smelled good, refreshing, Mommy noticed the flowers budding—a sign of hope, new life??? Maybe, maybe, someone will help—she pled inside, Mommy had no family-too many years of horror with her father, she ran away at 18-never to turn back. Now-nowhere to turn, no one to help her, no one to be there with her and a new baby.

She stares at her new pink maternity top, it's pretty-she longs to grow a new baby and fill it up. The car ride is quiet, eyes cast down as she cries and then she gives up and is quiet-she trembles. She remembers her last abortion-only 3 years ago, she tried to dismiss the thoughts but they hit her hard today. She remembers the pain involved, the sucking noises, the smells, the regrets after.

They park, she is screaming inside (so am I!) He pulls her in, reminding her of a better day tomorrow. He pays the $250 cash; they give her a number. A room full of quiet women-afraid.

The day is long, yet too quick for me as I say goodbye, as I leave into the arms of Jesus-I plead with her—don't cry, I'm with Jesus—full of joy and loving my Mommy. Please Mommy dearest don't give up the fight—keep fighting for babies like me—there are millions up here yes, my sister too. We know you miss us more than you can ever express—we long for you too, but we will be together soon.

A Wildflower Thrives in Florida

> *25 years ago, Mommy is still sad-thinking of what I would have been, looked like-she longs to hold me, love life with me! My name is Elizabeth*

Ten thousand days later, Ten thousand days ago

A familiar path

After my relationship with John collapsed, I returned to my old ways—partying and sleeping with as many men as possible. Deep down I was looking for "My Knight in Shining Armor" but there was no knight to be found, only my constant companion carrying a lance that pierced my own heart: that nagging sense of emptiness and longing. The desperation hit hardest at Thanksgiving, 1979.

My heart was the heaviest it had ever been. I was filled with grief and pain at losing John and also his family, who I loved. They were my family, the family I never had. I had spent all of my holidays with them for 5 years. I was part of them. So this Thanksgiving I decided to pump myself up and pretend everything was OK even though I was alone, poor and heartbroken.

That day I woke up and tried to "push back" the memories of my past, memories of what my family from Montana was doing that day with all the relatives I so loved. I thought of Aunt Fern who brought over food that always tasted bad but no one ever said anything because she was sure she was a good cook. I remembered my Uncle Tom (Fern's husband) who always reeked of alcohol and cigarettes but no one said anything as he stumbled across the living room. Aunt Alma would be there too, who was so much like Lucille Ball and made everyone laugh. I missed my grandma who was the most loving person I believe God ever created. She was "all love" and I ate up every ounce of her extravagant affection and compassion; she was my lifeline in the middle of the sexual and physical abuse.

My job as a kid on Thanksgiving was to get each family member a glass of wine when my mother finished preparing the dinner. I didn't know what a glass was, a little glass that is, and I would give them a large goblet instead. By the time my mother served dinner everyone was giggling and guffawing; I loved to watch them to see who would pee their pants from laughing so hard!!! It was a raucous Thanksgiving feast.

Well, that sad Thanksgiving, my family wasn't in my apartment but was together in Montana, whoopin' it up. I felt like the outcast because I had spoken up about the sexual and physical abuse and left home to save my life. Instead of relishing in my family's company I was alone with the pain. I turned on the radio to cheer myself up while I cooked my TV dinner. I blessed myself, thankful I had anything to eat, and took a few bites trying to convince myself it was just like my grandmother's cooking. Then I discovered an unwelcome guest: a big worm in my dinner. It was only half a worm but it didn't matter. I broke down into deep sobs. The pain from my lie-based thinking had me asking, "Why am I being punished God?" I called out through despondent weeping, "Help me!"

Your Time:

- Name five feelings you felt this week. Right now, just speak them out loud. What was happening at the time you felt each of them? Did you do anything to numb the feelings? If so, what?

- Have you ever had a "reprieve" from feeling alone and broken, like I felt when I was with John? But then you ended up with more trauma and damage, rather than being healed? Express that in words or drawings in your journal.

- What has gone wrong in your present circumstances that you think relates to past abuse?

Chapter 4

"Julie, I Love You"

Tragedy

AFTER EVERY FAILED ATTEMPT to find life, I would return to the little Wisconsin town where I started this new phase of life and to my best friend Cathy. "I haven't found it yet," she'd say. "But please don't give up Julie. I know something is out there. Will you still look with me?"

I kept looking, this time moving to St. Paul, MN, a city where I knew no one and had no attachments. I lived in a rundown little apartment, eating Wheaties for breakfast, lunch and dinner and scraping by on paychecks from my jobs at a bar and an insurance company.

I visited Cathy the week before my 21st birthday. We celebrated in our normal way—with drugs, alcohol and men. A week later I heard from Sue, a mutual friend. "Julie, did you hear about Cathy?" she blurted out over the phone. Before I had a chance to respond, Sue started choking with tears. "Julie," she finally started again, "Cathy's been murdered. While she was hitchhiking a guy picked her up and when they stopped, he shot her in the back."

Utterly stunned, I left my apartment and walked the streets of downtown St. Paul, weeping and searching desperately for an open church. I connected God with a church building. And for the first time in years I wanted to find God and pray. Cathy's death let loose a flood of questions. Is there even a God? Does He care? What happened to Cathy? Did she just disappear? Did she go to heaven? Did she go to hell? Unfortunately I didn't find an open church and I certainly didn't find any answers that night.

Rock at the bottom

Two days later I went to Cathy's funeral. It was so sad, all of her friends huddled around crying, without hope. That night we did what we thought would honor Cathy the most: we drank a keg of beer on her gravesite.

I went home after the funeral confused, wrestling with so many questions. Why did Cathy die? What is life all about? Is it just pain and nothing else? Why should I keep on living; it just hurts too much. I was poor, malnourished and an emotional wreck.

To cover the grief and pain I made a vow to myself: I would have a different bottle of booze and a different man every night. I kept up that vow very well. But one night I didn't have a bottle and I didn't have a man. I hit rock bottom.

I lay on my bed and began sobbing, not able to stop. All of the pain erupted like a volcano. I had placed a bottle of pills in the medicine cabinet for this "special" night when I would take my life. I took the pills out of the cabinet and started pacing around the room. Four times I put the pills back in, only to pull them out again.

I dug my long fingernails into my wrist, the skin raw and bloody, to divert my mind from the feelings of pain and hopelessness. I grabbed the pills and threw them in the waste basket to stop from committing suicide. After two hours, my body exhausted, I finally cried myself into a deep but troubled sleep.

In the middle of my deep sleep, alone in my one-room apartment, I heard a voice. Gradually growing louder and louder the voice kept repeating, "Julie, I love you; Julie, I love you; Julie, I love you." It was a strong and authoritative voice. I never even thought of questioning this person or asking, "Who are you?" At the same time, the voice seemed so calm, gentle and safe and I noticed comforting warmth rush over my body. I should have been afraid to hear voices in the middle of the night, but more than anything I felt loved and cherished.

I had no idea who spoke to me or where the voice came from. I certainly didn't associate it with Jesus Christ. And the words, "Julie, I love you" never really altered my circumstances, at least not immediately. But for two years every time my life felt hopeless that voice would come back, gently repeating, "Julie, I love you." I decided to make something better of my life.

Right turn

I applied to the University of Minnesota with dreams of becoming a teacher. During the admissions process, however, the career counselor warned me to give up those dreams. "Your ACT scores are so low," he warned, "that you'll never make it in college. You have skills as a secretary and a waitress, why not just stick with that?"

His words devastated me at first, but then this strength rose up in me and I became determined. I ignored his advice and kept pursuing that dream. For the next year I worked three jobs and took pre-college English, math and science. Finally, after a year of remedial courses, I started regular classes. Still lost and confused, not to mention exhausted, I was nevertheless surviving and moving forward.

I moved into a campus dorm for a time, working, studying and partying as much as I could. I didn't feel like I fit in very well since most students were younger than me and had money. By this point I had been away from home over five years and had already lived hard and fast. I had a few changes of clothing. I remember wearing the same jeans and shirts for years. I also had to work a lot harder than most students since I didn't have a mom and dad to depend on.

When holidays or spring break came around I got very depressed. Most students went home to family. I had no family so I spent holidays and vacations in front of the television with my TV dinner. I was very lonely and felt very "unwanted." I would try to pull myself up a bit by getting a new sun dress or reward myself somehow. Even for all I'd been through I still had some pluck and determination.

A different kind of family

During this time I waitressed at a small, local diner called Annie's Parlour in the Dinkytown section of Minneapolis. You meet a lot of people working in a restaurant. Most just come and go but then you have the "regulars" who seem to come in about the same time and order about the same thing every week.

One of my "regulars" was the Pedersons, Wayne and Norma, and their two daughters. They would come in Friday nights and order hamburgers and malts. I was curious about Wayne and Norma's relationship with their daughters. They didn't yell at their kids or hit them but were patient and loving with their girls. This was foreign to me. I was also intrigued how they treated me: they were loving and kind. They seemed to want to know me. This was surprising.

Those Friday nights waiting on the Pedersons touched me in an unexpected way. Someone who was pure and good liked me. And they wanted to be good to me. Why me? Would they still like me if they knew my past and my present? Deep down I felt like they would. I could tell they were Christians; I watched them pray before every meal and they spoke freely about God. At this point in my life I had met too many judgmental Christians who rejected me when they heard about my past. But this family seemed different.

Something inside of me changed when I met the Pedersons. I wanted to know them and people like them. I became curious about knowing God because these people followed God and I desperately wanted to be like them. Their lives spoke a new life to me; maybe I could have it too. Maybe, just maybe, my life could be pure and good.

Your Time:

- What does God feel like to you? Is He far or near? Strong or weak? What words would you use to describe God? Put it down in words or pictures in your journal.

A Wildflower Thrives in Florida

- In what ways have you been angry with God?
- Is God big enough to handle your anger?
- Do you remember the first time you had hope that your life could be different? How did that feel? What gave you that feeling?

Chapter 5

Something Amazing

Shiny girl

ALTHOUGH THE PEDERSONS HAD put a little hope in my life, I still walked around campus with my head bowed from shame and fatigue. Besides, on a huge college campus, strangers generally just avoid each other. One day, however, a bubbly girl about my age joined me as I walked to class and asked cheerfully, "Hi, my name is Michelle, what's your name?" Then she had the audacity to ask me how I was doing. And she actually meant it!

Midway into our conversation, Michelle casually said, "Oh, by the way, I'm starting a Bible study in my apartment. Would you like to join us?" *You're starting a Bible study?*, I said to myself. *Why would anyone get together and voluntarily study the Bible?* I had tried church once; it wasn't for me. Besides, I had formed my impressions of Christians. Christians were judgmental, aloof and perfect.

Everything in my head said, *No, I do not want to come to a Bible study.* But there was something different about this girl. She looked almost shiny, like she had this glow about her. I came to Michelle's apartment dressed in ratty jeans and a tight T-shirt. What does a person wear to a Bible study anyway? To my amazement, everyone looked rather normal. But even more startling, for the first time in my life I saw young men and women hugging one another and it wasn't sexual. I didn't think that was possible.

Someone handed me a Bible and helped me find something called 1 Corinthians chapter 13. Then those very normal-looking, friendly, hugging college students began reading the Bible. They spoke of love—not sex, not despair, not abuse, not performance, not fear—just love. They called it the love of Jesus. They talked about the cross and forgiveness in the same breath. They used strange phrases like being "born again" and "asking Christ into your heart." One or two shared how they had been "born again," how God had given them a "new start."

The words sounded strange, but God had prepared my heart for the concepts. At the same time, everything they said seemed completely inaccessible to me. My heart ached for the beauty of the love described in 1 Corinthians 13. But who was I to deserve that kind of love? "What if someone has done some really bad things?" I asked softly. *You people have no idea where I've been*, I thought to myself. *You have no idea of the sexual abuse, the promiscuity, the drugs and alcohol, the abortions, the suicide attempts, the godless despair.*

They confidently assured me that bad things didn't matter. "Jesus will accept you as you are," said one of the young women. A soft-spoken young man looked me in the eye and calmly said, "Julie, it doesn't matter where you've been. Christ can make you a new person tonight—even in this apartment."

So that night I accepted Christ in my heart. Michelle and her friends were ecstatic, hugging me and celebrating my decision. One of her friends talked about how the angels were dancing in heaven. I had no idea what that meant. I only knew that something deep and good had happened in my soul. For the first time in more than 15 years I felt clean inside.

A struggle upward

I had never felt so joyful. When I arrived at my efficiency apartment, I was still singing the songs from Michelle's Bible study!

Something Amazing

That night, for the first time ever, I slept peacefully. I didn't have the nightmares that had haunted me for years. I woke up the next morning so excited about life I felt I would burst.

For fifteen years I had lived on the edge, just trying to survive. It was a flat black-and-white world filled with pain and loneliness. Now the rich, multicolored beauty of God—the beauty I felt when exploring the mountains with Chico or lying in my grandmother's lap—came flooding back into my life. Only this time I knew the Source of that beauty. It was the same source that had called to me in the night: blessing me, wooing me, loving me. It was the voice of Jesus, the voice of my Beloved. The "something" that Cathy and I had tried to find had suddenly found me.

I danced to class and sang "Jesus loves me" all the way. It was the only Christian song I knew and everyone was going to hear it. I went to work at Annie's Parlour and started telling everyone about Jesus and how He saved me!

I told my co-worker Steve I didn't need drugs anymore because now I had Jesus. Steve, his eyes glazed by his typical marijuana high, stared at me with a mix of revulsion and awe. Obviously Steve had never heard of such a thing, but within two months he accepted Christ too. He wasn't the only one. Many people came to know Jesus in that restaurant because I couldn't contain my joy. I was the resident evangelist.

In the apartment below me there lived a kindhearted man named Tom. Five years earlier the doctors diagnosed Tom with multiple sclerosis and by then he was virtually confined to his wheelchair. Like me Tom knew despair and loneliness. So when I shared my story of faith in Christ he also received the hope and new birth Jesus offers.

I also learned something amazing in those first few months of new life. When I told Cathy's mother about my new faith in Christ, she quietly said, "Julie, you may find this hard to believe but the same thing happened to Cathy. Someone mailed me a small pamphlet that belonged to Cathy. Apparently she had read it and when it asked about giving your heart to Jesus, she signed her name and dated it. It was dated one week before her death." Jesus had "found" Cathy too! God constantly amazed me like this with his miraculous power and goodness.

Even though I experienced a dramatic turn-around, life was still hard. I still had to work hard to make it through school. I had a big battle with my addiction to alcohol and sex. I went to counseling and learned how to pray.

New life

A major turning point came when Michelle asked me to live with her. From a one-room efficiency apartment in a dilapidated building, she invited me to live in her 16th floor plush condominium. From eating leftover hamburgers and Wheaties, Michelle offered a fridge brimming with fresh fruit, chicken breasts, salads and pizza. From a wardrobe consisting of a few jeans and T-shirts, Michelle gave me beautiful "hand-me-down" dresses, blouses and slacks.

Michelle showed me daily how to be a Christian. She taught me how to dress, how to talk, how to pray and read my Bible. I started going to church with her. She introduced me to many of her friends who became my family.

But more importantly, Michelle demonstrated grace. She loved me unconditionally and adopted me like a sister. Nothing from my past even phased Michelle. She took me to church, taught me to read the Bible and told me about Christian music. She introduced me to a new world of friends, a world where love was more important than performance, intimacy was more important than sex, having fun was better than getting high, and praying was better than partying.

Jesus in the flesh

Michelle also told me about a Christian radio station because she knew I had this insatiable hunger for God and his words to me. As I listened one day I heard this man's voice that sounded familiar. Where had I heard this voice before? Oh my gosh! It was my

Friday night hamburger and malt regular, Wayne Pederson!!! That wonderful father and husband was also a teacher of God's word. I listened to him every day.

God loved me through Wayne's voice and his teaching. His program, New Dimensions, became my lifeline! I was very shy and didn't know if I could just call up the Pedersons so his voice became my connection to family. Maybe I could be a wife and mother someday. Maybe I could have a family like the Pedersons who were patient, kind and loving.

I listened to Wayne Pederson for years. When I did become a wife and mother I continued listening to him. His beautiful Scripture teaching became my home. He kept in touch with me and through the years has loved and supported me at some very critical moments.

Wayne and Norma Pederson have loved me so much in my life. They have truly become my adopted family and I am so very proud of them!!! I praise God for them and their God-touch in my life. I now have given that God-touch to my children (and hopefully others in my life that I minister to and love!)

Author and psychologist Diane Langberg says that recovering from trauma, especially abuse, hinges on a person who "incarnates the character of God" to the survivor. "They need somebody with skin on who will relate with them and be with them in a way that begins to teach them the truth about who God is by being that in the flesh," she says.[2]

Michelle and my church friends were Jesus in the flesh to me. Wayne and Norma have been Jesus to me too. Through these dear friends, in spite of human brokenness and sin, I saw Christianity in action. As one who never saw a godly home or marriage or parents, these mentors taught me about the faith. And even better, they showed me how to live as a Christian woman, mom, wife and child of God.

Your Time:

- Do you have anyone in your life who has been "Jesus in the flesh for you?" Name them out loud. How were they different?

A Wildflower Thrives in Florida

> How did they treat you?

- What are some of your symbols for God? I'm talking about images, icons and ideas that represent God to you. How about a tree, a house, a cloud, an ant, a frog? Any of those remind you of God? How has your perception of God been formed?
- Do you trust God? If you don't trust Him, why not? If you do trust Him, why?

CHAPTER 6

Old Reactions, New Reactions

Too much to handle

AFTER I BECAME A Christian and began growing in my faith, I wrote a paper for an English class at the University of Minnesota. It was very raw, telling my story in an exhaustive and detailed way. After my professor read it, she asked me to stay after class. She urged me to see a counselor at the university. That therapist saved my life in so many ways.

I'll never forget the first time I told this woman about my past abuse. She pounded her fist on the table and shouted, "This should never have happened! This was wrong." She had a heavy German accent, which, in my mind and emotions, gave even more authority to her strong, affirming words. Then she held me and let me weep.

By this time I had also been attending Michelle's church for a couple months. It was right before Easter. I wanted to know about Easter and celebrate Easter but I still wasn't sure if I had been completely forgiven for my past.

In addition to Sunday services I had been going to a college group at church. There were several hundred young people attending. They were like a family to me.

I decided to give my English paper to Sally, the leader of the college group. I was so nervous when I handed it to her. If she responded that God could forgive me, that there was grace and love, then I knew I had a chance that God would love me.

About a week later Sally was heading out for dinner and decided to stop by my apartment. She stood at the doorway and threw the paper at me. "I can't believe what you've done," the college leader said, her words full of disgust and anger. "You've had two abortions?! Your life is so messed up. I don't want to know you or even be around you."

She turned and marched away from my door. I was devastated, but being so new in my faith I resorted to old ways of getting through the pain. I went on a binge, riding my bike downtown, hitting the bars and getting rip-roaring drunk. I passed out in the street and somebody placed me in a church to sleep it off. I got up the next morning and rode my bike back to the apartment.

I didn't tell anyone what the college leader had said. I was afraid if they heard her words they might agree: I was too much to handle. I still went to the college group; they were too important to me. But I sat in the back where the leader couldn't see me.

Trying to understand

In spite of this experience, I continued attending the college group and going to church. I attended my first Maundy Thursday service that year (1980). For the first time in my life I heard the entire story of Jesus' crucifixion. As I listened with my ears, my heart, my whole body, I came to understand the pain Jesus suffered for our salvation. I also realized that Jesus, the exalted Son of God, mercifully understood my woundedness. Like me, Jesus had experienced great depths of abuse and rejection.

Psychologist Diane Langberg says this kind of experience is crucial for the traumatized. "[Change begins] when a survivor really begins to grasp, not just in a knowledge way but in an experiential way, that Christ has entered her trauma with her and experienced it also," she says. "That is the beginning of when you see Jesus take her by the hand and lead her out of the darkness into who she is in Him."[3]

As I wept quietly in the church pew after the service I didn't even notice the rest of the congregation had quietly filed out into the commons area. With bleary eyes and a snot-covered face (sorry, it wasn't a pretty scene), I found myself alone in the dark church. I was accustomed to crying alone, but on that night I wished someone would sit beside me.

Suddenly, on my right, I felt a hand placed gently on my shoulder. I turned to notice a young man who I knew from the college group and who I secretly admired, Matt Woodley. He was part of Michelle's group of friends. "If you want to, you can cry with me," he said softly. I didn't know it then but this was just the beginning of sharing sorrow and joy with Matt.

That Easter I celebrated the resurrection of Christ in church with my neighbor Tom and co-worker Steve. We stood side by side, listening with a deep spiritual hunger to the story of Christ's resurrection. We didn't want to miss a word.

As we sang "Christ the Lord is Risen Today," tears of thanksgiving streamed down our cheeks. We deeply appreciated, with a childlike acceptance, that because of Jesus Christ we were passionately loved and completely forgiven. And we knew that without Christ we would remain in a pit of despair.

Grace by the lake

Michelle continued to be Jesus in the flesh to me, along with many others. She brought me to worship services and to our church's college group. She stood by my side during retreats, campfires, hayrides, flamingo football games and group singing times.

Michelle also introduced me to Bonnie. I thought Bonnie was the most brilliant person I ever met. She would earn a Ph.D. from Princeton. She discipled me and taught me to love the Scriptures. But like Michelle, Bonnie gave me the greatest gift of all: unconditional love.

In the spring of 1981, Bonnie took me to northern Michigan to visit her family, the Godings. It was Bonnie's birthday and I watched with childlike awe as her family lavished her with gifts, a cake, songs and kind words. Trying hard to hold back the tears, I suddenly found myself quietly weeping at this display of lavish, overflowing love. Never in my 23 years of life had I experienced anything like this. I only had faint memories of my own birthday parties.

That night I went for a long walk along the shore of Lake Michigan. "Why don't I understand this love," I cried out to God. "Am I really that bad?" A deep despair came over me. "God, I'm not worthy of this love. Why do you tease me with it, placing it just out of my reach, when all along you know I'll never deserve it. These people are too good for me." I wanted to run and hide.

In my praying and wandering I lost my way and finally returned to the Godings. Based on childhood experience I expected rage for my tardiness. Instead they hugged me. "Julie, it's so nice to have you back," they explained. "We were so worried about you." Bonnie's 4-year-old nephew JohnDavid flew into my arms and with stuttering voice joined the feast of love. "I, I, I lovvve you," he whispered in my ear.

I grabbed him tight and buried my face in his shoulder and started bawling like a little girl. Bonnie's family surrounded me and hugged me some more. His sincere "I lovvve you" was one of the sweetest things I'd ever heard. I carried it in my heart for years to come. In a powerful way it was a constant reminder of God's unconditional love.

Something new

A year had passed since Matt sat with me after the Maundy Thursday service. I thought Matt was cute and smart but I was also afraid of him because I didn't feel good enough for him, even after he had let me cry on his shoulder. I just chalked it up to Matt being a kindhearted man caring for someone in trouble. So I was very much surprised when he approached Michelle to see if he could ask me out. She said "Yes" and Matt and I went on our first date.

Matt treated me like no man ever had. He had very strict boundaries when it came to being alone. He said he didn't want to be tempted. At first that kind of made me mad. That was the only way I knew how to relate to men and he wasn't interested in that part of me? What more did I have to give? He showed that I had much more to give and he wanted to get to know my heart and who I was. He even prayed with me. Wow, that was weird! But I also felt affirmed and loved by a man for the very first time. It wasn't about sex; it was about loving me for who I was.

Our romance was rocky in some ways as I began to understand this new way of relating. After two years we decided to get married.

Just before Matt asked me to marry him, he went to his spiritual mentor to ask for advice. Joe, a levelheaded, no-nonsense leader in our church simply commented, "All I can say Matt is I'm sure glad I married a virgin from a good Christian home." Matt had a deep respect for Joe but at least on this occasion he soundly rejected his advice.

Later Matt explained why: "It didn't ring true with the Gospel. If God can't change us, forgive us, redeem us, even in our brokenness, then what good is the Gospel? Is it only good news for perfect people from good Christian homes?"

God finds us in our brokenness and rather than walking away, he chooses us, cleanses us, binds up our wounds and then gifts us and calls us to share the good news with others. That was the heart of Matt's faith. We married Dec. 17, 1983.

Those early years of marriage were glorious. I was happier than I'd ever been in my life. I felt loved and safe. Instead of running from my past I was looking forward to the future, a future with children and a family life marked by joy, mutual respect and goodness.

Of course that didn't free our marriage from struggle. The wounds from my past sometimes haunted our marriage. The painful memories, the sexual flashbacks, the displaced anger, the deep grief that came in a hundred pieces, the strain with my family, my dark nights of depression—all of these added stress to our marriage. Matt struggled to understand the abuse, walking with me through the dark valleys, listening to my grief, allowing my sadness to come up without trying to fix me. Those early years were very healing for me.

I was not the only one dealing with damage from my youth. Matt had been exposed to porn at age 12 and never completely turned from it as a young man. This issue would haunt our marriage as well.

Your Time:

- What are some of the ways you are living out the consequences of your abuse? Where did you learn your beliefs about sexuality?
- Find a picture of yourself as a child and place it next to the book as you answer the following questions or finish the statements, inserting your name in the blanks:
    - This child, little _____, was sexually abused by . . . . ?
    - Little _____ was sexually abused because . . . ?
    - This child, little _____, was sexually abused at what age?
    - Did little _____ deserve the abuse?
    - If I were to adopt little _____, what would I tell her?
    - If I were to adopt little _____, I would . . . . ?

CHAPTER 7

Untangling the Past

New challenges

AS A VICTIM OF sexual abuse, I learned at a very young age to give sex in order to get love. It was a rule of relationships with men. This law governed my life for many years.

Of course, I didn't just make it up. This way of thinking was foisted upon me. After being sexually abused by my father, a neighbor man, an older co-worker, my uncle, my boss and a few others, I became a walking invitation for sexual abuse. So naturally, I thought that I deserved nothing better than abuse. Besides, if I wanted to find even a drop of love from a man I had to give away a little piece of my heart by having sex.

This attitude led me into a very promiscuous lifestyle. You remember my friend Cathy's challenge: every night drink a bottle of wine and sleep with a different man. I was addicted to sex.

Deep down, I knew I was looking for something besides sex. There was a gaping, hungry hole in my heart, a hole meant to be filled by God and pure relationships. But since I had neither, I snatched at the only thing I knew: to be held for at least a few minutes by a man, any man. I just wanted someone to hold me through the night.

After becoming a Christian and marrying Matt I swung to the other extreme. Sex became unpleasant, dirty, even disgusting.

I had flashbacks in which my husband literally became my abusers. In many ways this extreme was much more painful than the promiscuity, for I longed to give myself to my husband. Instead I was frozen and fearful. Those first few years of marriage were hellish at times because of these deeply negative reactions to physical intimacy.

Unraveling the pain and fear lurking under my sexuality was no small task. It took many years to understand the root problem went deeper than having or not having sex. There were profound issues of intimacy, trust, fear, sadness and longing for love. Christ had to bring his healing deep underground, way down into those wounded places in my heart.

Web of shame

There was a strong, destructive thread of falsehood that held my heart in bondage. I was a prisoner of shame. Whether promiscuous or frozen, I viewed myself as a sexual victim and misfit. I needed truth I could hold onto rather than the lies.

Professor and Christian psychologist Paul Singh says trauma survivors often have multi-tiered shame. What he means is this: they're afraid to admit they let this awful thing happen or they feel a profound sense of failure at not doing something about it. This doesn't mean those feelings are rooted in reality. Most survivors were helpless to prevent what happened to them.

Sexual abuse victims have emotions tied up in knots because, even though what happened was wrong and they were victimized, there were love needs being met in the midst of the abuse. Sharing these feelings of disgrace and humiliation in a group setting can help them untangle and release the shame. "When the fear of shame is disrupted, now the survivors can actually start to talk about the very thing that is a spiritual cancer in their spirits," Singh says.[4]

As God moved me further down the road of healing, the best advice I received was from a wonderful mentor, Jeanette Vought. Jeanette knew me and how I had messed up. She gave me emotional room to express the darkest parts of who I'd been, the way I thought, and the way I acted. Nothing was off limits. She also knew me well enough to recognize I would get through my sadness and fear and see joy tomorrow.

After opening my heart to her, pouring out my pain and dysfunction, Jeanette gently and confidently said, "Julie, never forget, this too shall pass." From her lips these words were more than just another Christian cliché. They were anointed, liberating words that stirred my hope. Thank you Jesus! I clung to her words because she loved me well and she also knew how God can totally heal someone.

The "shame disruption" Paul Singh describes began with Jeanette. I so respect her.

After dinner meltdown

When it came to forgiveness, I faced a real dilemma. Even as a baby Christian, I knew the Bible said you must forgive. Jesus didn't mince any words about it. He told us to pray, "Forgive us our trespasses as we forgive those who have trespassed against us." It really wasn't an option.

I had two major difficulties with forgiveness: 1) I didn't know where to start. After all, there were so many different pieces of the hurt, betrayal and rejection; 2) Even if I knew where to start I still didn't know how to do it.

Before I met Christ I never really forgave the people who hurt me, but then again, I didn't need to. I just numbed the pain by drinking, working and sleeping with men. Even still, the toll of unforgiveness and bitterness wreaked havoc with my health. I began having very bad stomach problems, which the doctor diagnosed as an ulcer when I was only 21.

Shortly after the diagnosis, I became a Christian and I began to learn about forgiveness, although I can't say I fared much better dealing with my issues. I wrestled with how to forgive this man who had sinned against me in the most painful way a little girl could ever experience. I wanted my father to pay for his sin against me! I was also very angry at my mother for not protecting me even though she knew what was happening.

Instead of my old damaging and wrong ways to cover the pain and anger, I found acceptable "Christian" ways of living in denial. I avoided the real work of forgiveness by minimizing the pain (it didn't really hurt that bad), by clinging to Christian clichés (God wants us to forgive and forget) and by trying real hard to be nice—even to my abusers.

This strategy worked for a while . . . until I started going crazy. Several years into our marriage Matt and I met my father for supper. Everyone was extremely pleasant. We talked about nice, safe things like the weather, the paper mill back home, real estate deals and the price of car insurance. As we ate our meal we just pretended the sexual and physical abuse had never occurred.

I tried so hard to be nice and pleasant that I went home and became violently ill, shaking and vomiting throughout the night. My emotions and thoughts spun around in a blurry, sickening whirl. *What if none of this ever happened?* I thought to myself. *Everyone else seems to deny the reality of what happened in my childhood. What if I made it all up and I'm really the crazy one?*

When I finally recovered about a month later, Matt and I learned an important lesson about forgiveness. Forgiving is not pretending. Forgiving is not acting like something never happened and therefore it couldn't possibly have hurt you. It is not an act of the will to ease an uncomfortable situation (i.e. "do the right Christian thing or be a good girl.") Actually, by trying so hard to pretend and be nice I found myself displacing my anger on others, especially the people I loved the most: my husband and children.

The confrontation

I gave birth to our first child, Bonnie Joy, in July, 1985. After she was born, I began having severe nightmares where my father broke into our home and sexually abused her as he had abused me. For a full year, I was afraid to sleep at night for fear she would be harmed. This may seem irrational to others because our apartment was safe, the doors were locked and my husband Matt was next to me, but to my unconscious mind I didn't feel safe.

We discussed these fears and also my meltdown with Dr. Nils Friberg, our godly counselor and mentor from Bethel Seminary. He suggested it might be time to confront my father with the sexual abuse I suffered at his hands. "Don't expect repentance, admission of guilt, reconciliation or even remorse," he warned us. "The confrontation probably won't bring healing to his soul or to your relationship with him. But it may bring a great deal of healing to your life."

So with many friends praying for us I got on one phone, Matt on another and we called my father to confront him with the sexual abuse. This was the fall of 1986. True to Dr. Friberg's words he denied all of it with much anger. How dare I accuse him of such a thing! We had offered grace and reconciliation, but it had to be a reconciliation based in truth, not denial. The offer was soundly rejected.

It may seem defeating that my father didn't own up to anything, but that confrontation released a huge burden from me, just as Dr. Friberg predicted. I had given the problem back to my father—it was no longer mine—and the nightmares stopped immediately. I felt like I could put my life back together and not live in tremendous fear any longer!

This freedom doesn't always happen with confrontation, but it happened for me because that little girl inside had a "voice." This voice allowed me to speak up for my own protection and for the protection of my children. I felt free at last!

I was able to confront reality, to revisit the pain and the abuse. Only this time it didn't confuse and overwhelm me. That was huge. I could sleep peacefully, freed from the frightening images that often haunted my dreams. The abuse and my abuser no longer controlled my mind.

The confrontation also knocked loose the emotional brush dam in my soul so God's love could stream through me to others. By acknowledging the abuse, feeling the hurt and expressing the anger, I could move on to the final steps of forgiving: letting go of my hatred and denial and embracing grace, for myself and others.

I became very intentional in forgiving myself and also those who had deeply betrayed me. I began to realize we cannot cheaply throw grace at victims and tell them to forgive the atrocities that happened. We cannot reduce forgiveness to a head exercise that leaves the one victimized dead emotionally. We need to face the damage—the real damage—and bring our broken hearts to God. He will help us restore peace!

Forgiveness is a process. It's the result of a conscious decision, usually many conscious decisions over time. It doesn't happen all at once. More often, it's like a journey with many steps. Just as God brings healing in bits and pieces, so forgiveness comes in bits and pieces as well. Rarely are there gigantic leaps forward.

Sometimes the choices to forgive seem difficult, painful, confusing, or even unfair. But they aren't choices to forget our devastation or excuse those who caused it or abolish boundaries to let those who hurt us back into our lives. For instance, we weren't going to trust our spirited little Bonnie with my dad. Forgiving is not trusting. But forgiveness is a choice to trust God with our pain, sadness and our right for pay back.

In our healing process we begin to come to terms with the imperfections of those who harmed us. The only perfect father is our Abba Father in heaven. But no matter how we calculate the losses and grief, we sadly come to terms with the truth that we can never be reimbursed for the damage done.

Ultimately forgiveness is a choice to follow Jesus. He desires that the traumatized, victimized and devastated move forward—past the offense and past the loss—into a full lifestyle of forgiveness. It's a choice to let go and bless our enemies, even if we have to set boundaries to protect ourselves. And ultimately it's a choice that will set us free.

Learning to be loved

My parents had been a source of distorted opinions that fed my distorted image. They told me they didn't want another child so I felt unwanted. And they also let me know they didn't want a girl, they wanted a boy. So I felt that since I was a girl that made me a bad person.

My mom and dad also told me I was stupid and ugly, so I felt like I didn't have any worth at all. I couldn't find anywhere in my life where I had worth. So I tried to be a boy; I wore overalls and worked really hard, cleaned the house, chopped wood and did all the things I was supposed to do because I wanted to be a boy.

My parents said I couldn't do anything with my life so I wanted to prove that I could. But marriage had calmed me down. I felt a level of security that I'd never known before. Matt was there for me. He comforted and encouraged me. My feelings of insecurity and fear abated. Matt's love helped me not feel so driven to push and make things happen.

But that dinner with my father unearthed something else. Matt had supplied a steadying influence in my life, but I came to realize I was looking for a strong defender and protector. Matt had been passive at dinner. Even when we decided to confront my father, I begged Matt to listen on the other phone when I called. He didn't want to step in.

I began to withdraw from Matt emotionally, turning aside when he tried to kiss me and closing my heart to his compliments and kind words. One day we were standing outside our house, preparing to go somewhere, and Matt finally blurted out, "Why won't you let me love you?"

What's wrong with me? I asked myself. *Matt's a good Christian guy. Why am I so uptight and cold toward him now?* I came to understand that both situations with my father made me feel unsafe with Matt. I wondered if he would ever really stand up for me or for our kids. But I also felt guilty for doubting my husband's love for me. Oh Jesus, why are we so complicated?

My mind kept going back to that evening. Matt had tried to make everything nice and OK when I felt he should have been confronting my dad. Why didn't he speak up for me? He knew what had happened? But then, we hadn't discussed having a confrontation with my father that night either. Shouldn't Matt have led that or at least questioned why we were having dinner with this man who had done such unspeakable harm to his wife?

Matt had a lot to learn about leadership but this situation raised serious trust questions for me. I know Matt was in over his head, but he also didn't show any effort to protect me. He didn't raise questions even about how we should be interacting with my father. I had been the one to stand up to my dad, to let him know he would not hurt me or my kids. I had to be the strong one.

It wasn't all about Matt. The Lord also showed me I was expecting of Matt what only my Heavenly Father could really provide. I had been reading John Eldredge's *The Sacred Romance* about the same time. "In all our hearts lies a longing for a Sacred Romance," John wrote. "It will not go away in spite of our efforts to anesthetize or ignore its song, or attach it to a single person or endeavor. It is a Romance couched in mystery and set deeply within us."[5]

God used this set of circumstances to turn my heart toward Him in a stronger and more intense way. He wanted me to learn to love and be loved by other human beings, but my first love should be Him. He will often cause circumstances to line up in order to break this bondage to lesser affections. He will turn our hearts toward Him, helping us find our true selves and true identity based on the Word of God and who we are in Christ. Would the Lord be my protector? Could I really believe that He would safeguard my children and me? Was I really His adored child or not?

As Jesus deconstructed my identity of victimization, he offered me a better way—identity as the beloved of God. Would I dare to believe that *nothing* can separate me from God's love—nothing that I could do or fail to do, nor anything that could be done by anyone else to me (Romans 8:31-39)? I had to go to Jesus for my strength and for my security. He could be my sacred romance; he could be my husband. I could feel safe with God. Out of this experience the Lord was asking me to lean into Him more completely. He was the best husband I could hope for.

Your Time:

- How do you respond when someone expresses that you have value? That you're worth loving? Take a minute and talk with God about that.
- What is the abuser responsible for? What did the abuser take away from you? What would you say to your abuser right now? Maybe the person who abused you is dead, or you're not ready to have that conversation. Write down what you might say, or express it some other way through song, drama or drawing.
- How did you feel towards your abuser? Did you feel like there was something wrong with you?

Chapter 8

Moving Experience

Growth and change

THOSE EARLY YEARS OF marriage were a time of tremendous change, both in terms of what God was doing inside me and how my external circumstances were changing. I earned a bachelor's degree in Christian education in June 1985 from Northwestern College, just a month before I delivered Bonnie Joy. We welcomed our second child, Mathew, in 1987.

Matt graduated from Bethel Seminary in June, 1989. A month later we moved from St. Paul to the quaint farm town of Barnum, MN where Matt served as senior pastor at Barnum United Methodist Church.

I also graduated from Bethel in 1990, with an associate's degree in theology. This was an incredible time of personal transformation for me, mainly because of one woman: Dr. Jeannette Bakke. Jeannette was a strong force of God's love for me in incredible ways. She met with me to offer spiritual direction. She also helped me plan a memorial service to mourn for dearly loved relatives who had died while I was away from Montana.

God handpicked Jeannette to speak deeply into my heart and show me that God's love is true, right, and profound and that He had great plans for my life. I reflected on her words when I was mothering, when I so desired to be a great witness for God and when I began to experience a deep mystical part of my spiritual heart that no one could explain to me nor did I have the courage to tell them. She became the voice and heart of God for me.

This wasn't the end of change for me, but the beginning. We added JonMichael to our family, born February, 1990. I delivered Wesley, our fourth and last baby, in May, 1993. I also earned a master's degree in counseling in May 1993 and opened a counseling practice that fall in Duluth, about 40 miles north of Barnum.

Those were wonderful days for my family and me. I had moved from being a devastated receiver of grace to someone who could pour time and love into others in need. And now I was a college graduate—not once but three times! And all this after I'd been told to give up my dreams of college. To say this was a miracle seems obvious, but I'll say it anyway: I was living a miracle! Jesus is a wonder worker. He changes lives from the inside out.

Two others

My first abortion was initiated by my parents. They wanted to avoid the embarrassment of a pregnant teenage daughter. The second abortion was initiated by my boyfriend. He wanted to avoid "inconveniences" as he pursued his political aspirations.

It seemed like everyone in my life considered abortion the ideal solution to personal problems. As a young woman I did too. When I was in my early 20s I believed in abortion so much that I volunteered at the oddly named Family Tree, a small clinic that advised young women to "terminate" their pregnancies. After all, wasn't this just freedom of choice? That's what I thought then.

When I accepted Christ, God changed my heart. Deep down I always knew that abortions were wrong. The church told me it was wrong. Abortion is murder, they said. I got the message loud and clear and I knew it was true. But I also carried a burden of guilt and grief that nearly broke my heart. How could I release that burden and rest in Jesus' loving arms?

Shortly after my conversion I tried to share this burden with the college ministry leader at the church. I gave Sally my English essay, which openly shared my past: the sexual promiscuity, the two abortions, the guilt, the shame, the longing for forgiveness and healing. You know how that went—she threw the paper in my apartment and said she didn't want anything to do with me.

That experience alone was enough to push my shame and guilt underground . . . deep underground. I kept it buried for nearly 15 years. And it didn't surface until our fourth child, Wesley, was about 1 year old. One pleasant summer afternoon as I watched all four children playing on the beach—running, giggling, splashing in the shallow water and loving life—it suddenly occurred to me I actually had two more children, two children I had aborted.

The grief hit me once again and I knew I had to risk sharing it with someone. I couldn't carry it by myself anymore. I had to do something to face it out in the open.

The next year I planned and participated in an event called a Reconciliation Memorial Service at a Catholic church in Duluth, Minnesota, right next to Lake Superior. It was a day set apart to process the guilt, shame, fear and grief from my two abortions. And best of all, it was a safe place: a place for truth and grace, a place to be held in God's loving hands.

There were 10 of us grieving the children we'd aborted. At first I stayed in coordinator mode and didn't want to surrender to the process of facing my loss. I fought it. Two friends took my clipboard away and allowed me to just heal and experience the presence of Christ. It was so hard. I bonded with two baby dolls they gave me. I felt God gave me the sex (two girls) and the names—Ruth and Elizabeth—of my two daughters.

At the end of the healing day we were to lay our baby dolls down in a bassinette to give to Jesus but it was way too hard. I bonded so much I couldn't let the baby dolls go. The lady on the left of me had seven abortions and the woman on the right had four. We were all wailing in pain!

I knew that unhealed abortion wounds are a great burden, but I had no idea how heavily they had weighed on me. After all, my first abortion had been nearly 20 years earlier. Body-shaking sobs of grief rocked me like an earthquake. I thought the stream of pain and tears would never end. I looked up and begged God to help us. We couldn't seem to forgive ourselves.

Then, all of a sudden, the children's choir upstairs began to sing "Jesus Loves Me". It was so surreal. We all looked up through our tears and knew this was from God. We then had the freedom to lay our babies down and give them to God. All of us left there filled with such joy!!! We all were lighter—and so happy. This was truly a miracle from God. After being bound by guilt and grief for 20 years Jesus broke the chains and set me free.

Flood

Sexual abuse damaged me and distorted my soul. There were many wounded places in my heart, places of loss and great sorrow. Unfortunately, because I spent so much time just struggling and getting by, I never had time to mourn what was lost.

I eked by in survival mode, even as a believer in Jesus. Only now I survived in Christian ways: doing ministry for God, sharing my testimony, attending workshops and conferences and running to church meetings. But underneath, I was operating by the same core principle: *it's too scary to face your heartache so run with all your might.*

Then the running came to an abrupt halt. Not because I wanted to stop, mind you. I stopped because God brought me to the ocean inside. There was nowhere else to run. Like the sea, my grief was impossible to miss. That ocean of despair washed over me for more than a year.

In 1997, Matt was offered the post of senior pastor at Cambridge United Methodist Church in the small town of Cambridge, MN. I know many people change jobs and make moves. I had moved a lot as a young woman, trying to run away from my past.

By this time, things had changed. I was putting down roots and God had grown our family and my career. This is no reflection on Cambridge or the church, but this transition brought an end to a very precious phase in my life. I left almost everyone behind: friends, the counseling center, my ministry. Worst of all,

Matt didn't really consult me about this career change, but moved forward without discussing it. This had a ripping effect on my soul. In many ways it was like leaving home all over again. I felt like that frightened, lonely 18-year-old girl who was boarding the train at 4 a.m. and leaving everything behind. I was devastated.

For a year I fell into a deep depression. All that unresolved pain and soul anguish came bubbling to the surface. Even though I knew the hope of Christ, my heart felt bereft of hope. The sadness and grief kept pouring out and there was no end in sight.

The bubbling turned into an uncontrolled torrent. God opened a floodgate of grief. I started replaying scenes from my childhood, scenes of abandonment and rejection. For the first time, I felt the full force of that teenage girl's sorrow. After years of avoidance I had finally tapped into it, allowing myself to feel it and let it stream out of me.

Obviously this wasn't my idea of healing. I felt I was moving backwards instead of forwards. I couldn't speak except to pray. In 3 months I lost 50 pounds, shrinking from a size 12 to size 0.

At my lowest point, the day of my 39th birthday, I prayed for some sign of hope. That morning a friend arrived with a dozen long-stem white roses. God responded to my prayers so beautifully. The turnaround took another six months of slow healing but God was faithful and he brought me out.

What ultimately helped me heal? What pulled me out of the depression? There was no shortcut, just a decision of faith to trust God and embrace the grieving process. Instead of blocking the immense sadness or trying to dodge it, I let it sweep over me.

I believe this entire year was a delayed and prolonged reaction to the sadness in my heart. I realize that medication may have helped me during this process as it has helped many people. But deep down I knew I had to do everything in my power to walk through the pain and not around it.

I learned something very important that year: the pain of suffering can't be dammed up forever. It always finds a way to seep into the present, no matter how hard we try to keep it plugged up. Healing from pain involves learning to recognize, experience and share emotions rather than denying or suppressing them. It is important to express these emotions in a safe environment—like a support group or with a therapist.

This will reduce the depression and anxiety that these emotions may carry and help us regain control over our lives. Then we can move through the waters safely, knowing we have others to help us out.

God's healing work in my life isn't done. There will be more sadness and grief. But now I know that it's healthy and normal to grieve; I don't feel ashamed of my sadness anymore. Sometimes we need to stand at the cross and hurt. For it's at the cross that our wounded hearts receive God's intricate and pervasive healing.

Near the end of this prolonged period of mourning and divine heart work, I picked up John Eldredge's book *The Sacred Romance,* the same book I'd begun reading about the time of the confrontation with my father. Have you ever read a book and felt as if the author had written just for you? That's how I felt about *The Sacred Romance.* "Lord, this man gets my walk with You," I said out loud. "He understands the romance I've had with you all these years. Please God, I would love to meet him and work with him."

Within a month I was speaking on the phone with Morgan Snyder, John Eldredge's assistant. I was so thrilled!!! John and Morgan were planning a Sacred Romance conference for Minneapolis. They had heard I worked with a counseling center and also with radio station KTIS. So I was invited to help plan this conference. What a miraculous, speedy answer to my heart's longing.

Planning the conference took a year and a half and was a constant walk of faith. First, we couldn't find a church to host the event because, at that point, no one was familiar with John. By the time of the conference in January, 2002, John's name was very well known in Christian circles. We prayed that every seat would be filled in the 1,801–seat auditorium and that we'd not have to turn anyone away. And, just like God, he provided 1,801 participants for the conference.

Every step of the planning process John and Morgan showed me how to listen to the voice of God and to sense his nudgings.

That meant so much to me, especially after the time of trial I had just endured. They continued to support and love me afterwards and have often spoken the voice of God into my life. They supported the In the Wildflowers DVD project, with John serving as host. Both men have been so instrumental in my Christian walk and in teaching me to follow God by faith. They have sent me flying with faith, hope and love!!! What an incredible team they have with their ministry Ransomed Heart. I thank Jesus so much for these two godly men.

Your Time:

- Have you developed psychological ways to stay away from the pain of shame? What are they?
- What are some shame messages that you believed? By shame message I don't mean guilt, which is related to wrong moral decisions or actions. A shame message is a statement of self-contempt, a wrong and negative message that devalues your worth as a human being. For instance, one of my shame messages was, "You're so messed up you'll never be able to love or be loved."
- Have you ever thought, "I'll just forget about it, it will go away" about your trauma? That wrong idea impacted me deeply. How has it affected you?

CHAPTER 9

Higher and Deeper

Beyond words

I'VE SEEN AND DONE and experienced many things in my life, many tragedies, many joys and many sorrows. But visiting Ground Zero took me to a whole new level. There was nothing to say.

I think it was the hand of God that brought us to New York almost three months before September 11, 2001. My husband had been pastoring a church in Minnesota but through a chain of amazing events he was offered the post of senior pastor at a church in the New York City area. So we left Cambridge, MN, all six of us, and headed for the East Coast.

We moved into the church parsonage—a large, seven-bedroom Victorian style home, which was overwhelming all by itself. For a bunch of Midwesterners, New York was a big adjustment—the food, the energy level, just the whole feel of a city that is like a world in itself. And then tragedy hit and it hit in a way that touched the whole world.

Eight days after 9/11, I was serving McDonald's food to rescue workers and policemen and firemen about a block from Ground Zero. It was surreal and disorienting. We handed out hamburgers and Cokes to people who were digging through tons of rubble, listening for the slightest hint of someone alive in the midst of the destruction. Grieving family members were there too, hoping for some encouraging word.

One day armed soldiers took us near the base of Tower 2. We went to support those in the middle of the rescue efforts. I remember standing there transfixed as workers gathered near a place where they hoped for a sign of life. They listened for any kind of sound—knocking on metal, moans or groans, yelling—anything that meant someone was still alive.

The circle of people listened intently but heard nothing. It was both a beautiful and bittersweet thing to watch. I started feeling ashamed because I'd brought a camera. But this scene was just too personal, too intimate and sacred. It wouldn't have been right to snap a photo there.

While I was working at the base of Tower 2, a piece of glass sticking out of the ground ripped through my pants and cut my leg. I was bleeding but not a whole lot, but when I looked up I was surrounded by firemen and rescue workers. Wow! One guy tore his shirt and wrapped the material around my leg. I thought to myself: *What a response! They were looking for life and I was someone they could help who was alive.* It was shocking in a positive way to see how they wanted to give.

More than anything else, I felt surrounded by love. Here were hundreds and hundreds of volunteers searching desperately for friends, co-workers and strangers. Many hadn't slept for days. But there was no sacrifice too big if they could find somebody and in some small way redeem this horrible event.

The scene at Ground Zero changed me. I knew that I had seen a larger kind of love going on there. In the midst of soul-breaking sorrow, people gave their all for the sake of others. In spite of the tremendous despair I saw hope. I came away grateful and wanting to be, more than ever before, a source of healing for others.

Cancer

It was fall, 2002. I was in the midst of filming a DVD series on general trauma for Restoring the Heart Ministries, the non-profit organization I founded. Our film crew had just shot footage at the site of the World Trade Center. Our family had settled into the New York City rhythm. Life was going so well.

I pushed away any concern about the lump in my throat. I had a good cancer doctor in Minnesota who examined it regularly over the course of 9 years. He had never ordered a biopsy so I thought it was fine. But that fall I visited a gynecologist and asked him to check the lump. He insisted that I get it looked at right away by an oncologist.

The oncologist ordered a biopsy immediately. What a painful procedure. The technician should have put me to sleep. Instead I was awake through the whole dreadful process while he poked me over and over trying to collect enough fluid.

As bad as the biopsy was, the outcome was worse—yes, it was thyroid cancer. Oncologists call this the best cancer to have because it often stays contained to the throat. But it had spread to my lymph nodes and around my vocal chords so I really didn't know what my future held.

This diagnosis shattered my world. Because they didn't know how far the cancer had spread, my fears of the unknown ran rapid. I would sit by my children's bedsides at night weeping, listening to them breath. "What if I don't get to see them grow up?" I wondered aloud. "I want to watch every step of their lives Lord. Please, please, let me live."

At first I asked, "Why?? Why this assault Lord??" But this conversation just made me frustrated. So I began to ask, "What? What Lord, would you like me to do with this chapter of my life that is so unknown?" An incredible peace came over me as I began to lean into God and not fight Him in this battle. I knew the Lord would lead me on this road as He has so tenderly led my whole life.

I read so many Bible verses at this time; over and over I would drink them up, longing to be filled with the hope they described. Often I read Isaiah 35:4-6, "Say to those who are fearful-hearted 'Be strong, do not fear! Behold, your God will come and save you . . .' Then the eyes of the blind shall be opened, and the ears of the deaf shall be unstopped. Then the lame shall leap like a deer, and the tongue of the dumb sings. For waters shall burst forth in the wilderness, and streams in the desert" (NKJV). This one phrase became my victory refrain: "Be strong, and do not fear!"

Depressed to blessed

The surgery to remove my thyroid was difficult. I remember getting ready for surgery, taking my clothes off, putting on the gown and thinking, *What happened to my life?* I was afraid of how I'd look after the surgery with two large incisions in my neck: one cut across the bottom to remove the thyroid and another one up and down to remove the lymph nodes. I knew I'd look like a mess.

When I woke up from surgery I was very sick to my stomach. How painful to throw up with the huge incisions on my neck. I wasn't able to feel the right side of my face or walk much. Everything at that time felt "black." I was depressed and very down.

Everyone was so shocked when they saw me. I was so very weak and couldn't talk or walk. My children were afraid to look at me when I got home. They called me "bobble head" because I couldn't keep my head up and I had a big drain coming out of my neck.

It took several months to recover from the surgery and then I had to go on this crazy diet where I couldn't eat any sodium for 4 weeks—not one ounce! Everything has sodium in it! Then I had to go off Synthroid, a drug that helps regulate your body's energy level. So over two weeks I kept getting weaker and weaker. By the end, I needed help to walk because my body was virtually "asleep." I could feel it go to sleep starting at my fingertips and toes, that tingly numb feeling working its way through my whole body.

I prayed over and over during this scary bend in my road that I would learn to "suffer well." I prayed that I would find true hope and that as God shattered my dreams He would create in me an appetite for better dreams, dreams that are from my Father. My Heavenly Father had always faithfully taken care of this daughter. In an incredible way, I found my deepest worship in my tears.

Higher and Deeper

I slowly learned how to adjust to the constant weakness and the limitations. I began to see my limitations as a way to focus on the things of God. Instead of having a scattered chaotic life, I needed to be very intentional about what God was calling me to do each day. I began to get glorious glimpses of God in everything I did, people I encountered on the streets of New York, older people in the grocery store that appeared frail.

I began to reach out in my weakness with the hands and love of Christ. My weakness became a great opportunity to love the broken. It may seem incredible but I began to thank God for it! This is what He can do if we let him.

Science fiction

On my 45th birthday I went through radiation, another crazy process that required me to stay in a hospital room wrapped in plastic so I didn't contaminate anyone. A man came into my room wearing what looked like a space suit, bringing a container that smoked from liquid gas. He would then hand me a pill with a foot long pair of tongs. And I had to put it into my mouth!!! I thought I was in a science fiction movie. For the next week I had to flush the drug out of my system with liquids, showers and going to the bathroom a lot.

I was in isolation for 10 days. This was a very lonely time. I couldn't talk on the phone because I would contaminate the phone. I couldn't read a book unless I threw it away after I was done with it.

I learned to laugh a lot in those times and my children laughed with me, sometimes between tears. Someone gave me Brennan Manning's article "Shipwrecked at the Stable." That's exactly how I felt: shipwrecked. I was poor in spirit, just like Manning writes, adrift on the open sea, clinging with a life-and-death desperation to the one solitary plank. And I prayed that when I washed ashore that I would be stripped of the old spirit of possessiveness in regard to anything except the glorious love of my Savior.

I realized we don't have a Savior who casually waves to us from the shore in these storms of life, watching in an entertained way as we flounder in our little pathetic worn-out sea boats. No, we have a Savior that gathers up His robe and jumps right into the water and rescues us, holds up our heads and does not let us drown, even though we wonder at times if the waves will overtake us. Our Lord is not aloof. He is active, He is loving, and He boldly helps us when we are drowning.

Celebration with friends

I had gotten to know many patients from the radiation department. We had come to love each other and had cried together. Some were very weak from cancer, others devastated by a diagnosis. I felt like the chaplain of the group as I prayed for many of them.

On Christmas Eve, 2002, I went in for my body scan. And guess what? No cancer! That was the best Christmas present I could have ever received. And the doctor announced the wonderful news as I was sitting with all of these beautiful people: "Julie Woodley is cancer free!" They all shouted with joy and hugged me (even though they weren't supposed to). I was overjoyed but also sad for them; why couldn't they have such a Christmas present too? I held back the tears but cried and prayed for them when I left the hospital.

I went home, my body very swollen from an allergic reaction to the radiation drugs. My face blew up like a balloon! I didn't care—I was alive!!!

Your Time

- Pain is a regular part of human life. Will you allow Christ to lead you out of the pain of your trauma into joy? Do you have a wall between you and God? What does it look like? Can you illustrate or describe it?
- Sometimes pain is very shocking, as in the aftermath of sexual abuse, or in the middle of a severe illness. Sometimes we have so much pain we become numb, unable to feel. Can you release your pain to God right now?

Chapter 10

Raining and Pouring

Not a beauty mark

I HAVE TO BE checked every year by a dermatologist because I am so fair and my mother allowed me to be very, very burned as a child. I always seemed to have blisters on my skin and had fainted a few times from the sun. I had just had a checkup with the dermatologist and he said I had no spots that were a concern. But I was looking in the mirror one day at a spot under my nose, that the doctor said was a "beauty mark." The mark had changed. I felt God saying, "Get this checked out right now," so I called up the doctor to make another appointment.

The receptionist said that I had just been in and unless it was skin cancer I would need to pay for the appointment out of pocket because insurance wouldn't cover it. I told her I felt like it was cancer and needed to come in regardless. I'm glad I listened to God because again it was cancer. What a blow! I had just recovered so this took a mental and emotional toll on me out of proportion to the nature of the disease.

This time I went through a five-hour surgery where I was awake. They kept scraping the skin and testing to see if it was cancer. They had to keep digging because it was so deep. I am a big bleeder so there was a lot of blood and they had to keep cauterizing the wound.

I went home a mess again. My face was huge! My kids again made silly fun of me. They said I looked like a monster. I went in the next day for a four-hour plastic surgery to repair my lip. It took about two weeks for my face to go down because it was so swollen and about a year before my lip began looking somewhat normal. But once again, it all didn't really matter, because I was alive.

Road kill

Two years after the initial diagnosis of thyroid cancer my body was healing and I felt a surge of energy I hadn't felt in some time. We had moved out of the church parsonage into a new home in a quiet neighborhood. After dinner one night I decided to take a bike ride while Matt took our youngest son to soccer.

I felt alive again—the warm air rushing by my face, the smell of salt air from the ocean beach which was my destination. I peddled the one mile there without a problem and headed back. But as I neared our new home I heard the chink of metal hitting metal. The bike chain had fallen off and wedged in my pedal.

The bike stopped almost immediately like I'd run into a brick wall. I flew off my bike, thrown forward as if by slingshot, and skidded on the asphalt. I don't remember the accident at all but I injured my head, right elbow and scraped up my knees and forearms very badly. I was a bloody mess, unconscious and crumpled in the middle of the street.

Thank God one of our new neighbors found me just a few minutes after the accident. He was my Good Samaritan, wrapping my body in a soft blanket and calling for emergency help. Matt and Wesley drove into the plat as the rescue crew loaded me in the medic.

I was such a mess. My elbow was broken, cheek bone cracked and there were many cuts and scrapes. But that wasn't the worse. I had also suffered a hematoma and brain hemorrhage. I felt dizzy and run down for months. I had to relearn basic things like walking and speaking in understandable sentences. Even for all that I have no memory of the accident. But someone else did.

Raining and Pouring

I mentioned Matt and Wesley showing up just as I was being carted away. They made their way past police tape toward our house. They weren't sure what had happened but when Wes saw blue shoes on the street he knew they were mine. Suddenly he realized the unconscious hurt lady on the stretcher was his mom. The fear he felt was overwhelming and he didn't know how to translate his emotions into words.

Wes didn't say much about the accident or how it touched him for six months. But one day it just spilled out like fizzy soda from a shaken two-liter bottle of pop. That day he and I were almost in a car accident. Out of nowhere he began crying loudly. "Mom, you don't understand!" he spoke out suddenly. "I saw those shoes and I thought you were gone." All that hurt and fear poured out of him.

I was glad Wes finally spoke up. From personal experience I knew how important it was to bring those feelings to the surface. "The losses of adult life may actually be compounded by some of the unresolved losses of our childhood," says psychologist H. Norman Wright. "These are brought into adult life like unwelcome baggage. And in time, this baggage could turn an adult loss into a crisis."[6]

Wesley remembers

The following is an English paper Wesley wrote about that awful day. I am so glad to be able to share this honest and very personal sharing from my son's heart:

I still remember the day my Mom had her accident like it was yesterday. It was a beautiful Tuesday night right after I finished practice for my club soccer team. After practice my dad was waiting for me outside as he did after every practice. Besides an off feeling in the pit of my stomach, the day seemed completely normal and nothing out of the ordinary was happening.

On the ride home my Dad and I discussed how my day was and how practice was as we did after every practice, but as we turned the corner onto my street time started to move very slowly. As my Dad slowly turned the wheel of our 1993 blue Volvo, I noticed something around the corner that didn't belong and that I wasn't used to seeing on my quiet suburban street. Instead of there being a soundless, boring street, the entire road was filled with ambulances and cop cars. You could hear the sounds of all the vehicles from a mile away.

When I first saw all the ambulances and cop cars I thought it was one of my neighbors or, worst case scenario, one of my brothers who broke an arm playing soccer in the street. Immediately after we turned the corner onto my street we were stopped by a police barricade. My father jumped out of the car and ran up to the barricade to see what the situation was. The police officer told my dad that someone had fallen off their bike and was in critical condition. My father let out a sigh of relief, not knowing it was someone in our family.

As my dad turned away to go back into the car he caught a glimpse of the injured person from the corner of his eye. It was my mom! Dad sprinted past the police barricade and shoved policemen and ambulance workers out of his way, left and right, in order to get to my mom's side. I was completely shocked and instead of running to my mom's side with my dad to comfort her and see how she was doing I continued to sit in the car frozen with disbelief.

After a couple minutes of pure confusion and trying to build up my strength to get out of my car, I swallowed my fear and slowly creaked open the passenger's door and made my way towards mom. I had never felt a daze like this before; I felt like a man making his way to his own execution. I continued to slowly walk towards my mom and each step felt like an eternity as I began to see her outline between the parade of ambulances blocking my street. I passed by dozens of cops and ambulance workers and each of them stopped what they were doing and stared at me slowly walking as if I had some sort of disease.

I finally reached the side of my mom and kneeled next to her and immediately began to weep. As she lay there, she looked lifeless; I didn't know what to do. There was already a pool of blood pouring out of her head and down the street. I was again frozen with terror and disbelief. One of the ambulance drivers picked me up; I don't think he wanted me to see my mom in that condition.

The worker quickly began to ask me questions about my mom to distract me, but every question he asked I couldn't answer because I was so focused on my mom's well-being. They told me she would be fine as they secured a neck brace on her and slowly loaded her onto one of the ambulances. Their words gave me no relief because I knew they always say these things no matter the condition of the victim.

As I turned to see all the ambulances and cop cars leaving I began walking back to my house to wash the blood off my hands, which got there from stroking my mother's hair trying to wake her up. Inside my house my brothers and their friends were sitting in the living room playing video games like nothing had happened. I was so mad. They didn't know it was mom but they didn't even bother to go outside to see what the ruckus was about. They just kept playing their game. My dad talked to me and assured me everything was going to be OK and I calmed down a bit. I laid in my bed and got some much needed rest.

After I woke up, my dad told me I could visit my mom in the hospital. I was really happy about seeing her so when I got to the hospital, which I hate, I ran to the front desk to find her room number. I was expecting to see my mom smiling and excited to see me, but when I walked into her hospital room it was not what I had expected. My mom lay in her bed as if she was lifeless with tubes coming out of everywhere.

Although this was a very traumatizing time in my life, it showed me how precious life is and how it can be taken away from you at any second. This also taught me that, before my mom was in this accident, there were times I hadn't treated her with the utmost respect the way you should treat a loved one. On the other hand this incident helped me love her like I should and taught me to treat her well from now on.

My siblings and I grew up without showing very much respect to our parents and we would yell at them or tell them to "shut the hell up" with little or no consequences at all. Everyone thought that since we were a pastor's family that we had everything put together and we had no problems, but it was the complete opposite. My family had problems every day. Just a couple of days before my mom's injury we were having another one of our screaming fights about something that I can't remember at the moment, but I'm sure it was something stupid like me staying up late or doing my homework.

When she had her injury the only thing I could remember was how badly I treated her and how I was going to have to live my entire life with that regret nagging at me. Although my mom and I still have occasional fights about stupid things, from that point on after her injury I have learned to treat my mom the way an amazing mother ought to be treated.

My mom has gone through more traumatic injuries than anyone could possibly imagine and instead of feeling sorry for herself or sulking around, she took these instances and grew stronger and is now one of the most amazing and strong women I have ever met. All of my siblings had gone through life not respecting our mother and talking to her as if she was just another kid. We never treated her the way that sons should treat a mother, especially one as good as she is.

Just a couple weeks before my mom got into her accident we got into a big fight. She was just trying to get me to do a couple easy chores around the house, but I was never very good at obeying what my parents told me to do. She started yelling, then I started yelling and in the end I told her that I wished she was never my mom and wanted her to just leave. At the time I didn't think twice when I said it but after her accident I felt awful about it and swore then and there that I would always treat my mom the best I could and be a better son.

Sometimes in life it takes a terrible accident like this one for you to realize how precious life is and how you need to treat your family and loved ones as if it is their last day. Sometimes it takes a smack in the face for you to start treating the people who mean the most to you the way they deserve to be treated.

Your Time

- Have you ever had an experience that was a wake-up call to people you love? Perhaps you had a dissociative episode where you forgot who you were. Or maybe you had an accident that landed you in the hospital. How did their response affect you?
- How have the losses of childhood followed you into adulthood? One of the losses from sexual abuse is childhood, that you never really experienced one. Have you grieved that loss? Has that little child inside really been allowed to face and process that loss?
- Where was God in your trauma? That's one of the questions believers in Jesus must wrestle with. How has he met you after your trauma?

Chapter 11

Bridges to Healing

Healing words

My bike accident, which followed a nasty bout with thyroid cancer and basil cell cancer, resulted in severe brain trauma. I had to learn how to walk and talk all over again! Aspects of life that I never considered exceptional now required exceptional effort to regain. I felt miserable, bewildered at having to relearn how to walk normally and talk clearly. My motivation was at an all-time low. I'm usually very energetic and ready to meet the day, but my body and my heart were very badly beaten.

It was a painful time in many ways but also a joyful time. Every breath was a continual praise to God. The uncertainty of life moved me more deeply into the certainty of Jesus' love for me.

During this time, a precious friend began sending a daily devotional on email. I could sense the compassion of the Lord as I read each one, as if the Spirit himself was washing over me, cleansing me and pouring hope into my soul. I needed that so much. Those daily devotions inspired me to get up and start each day.

Several years later, with the pain of that physical and emotional recovery still fresh in my heart, I attended the American Association of Christian Counselors conference. Walking through the exhibit hall I saw a sign that grabbed my attention: Lighthouse Network. This was the source of those wonderful ministering words I received when I was rehabilitating! Praise you Father! As I approached the booth I began weeping. Through sobs of joy I told the man how much those devotions meant to me and he explained that he was Karl Benzio, the author of those inspiring messages. I was just floored! "You so restored my life," I told him. Jesus has been so good to let me make personal contact with people whose words have healed me. Thank you Lord!

Hero in the cancer ward

My almost-death experience made me so aware of how broken we all are. We all are the "walking wounded," in the spiritual sense. We all carry physical and emotional injuries that differ in level of pain. We often try to escape our pain in not-so-good ways. When life has turned us upside down and thrown us all around we just want to find comfort and peace.

If we focus only on escaping our pain we may start a dangerous cycle of addiction. We become loyal to our "false gods." That was a hazard for me. And then I met a wonderful man who had brain cancer. He went through numerous surgeries to remove his brain tumor and would go in and out of consciousness after each procedure. I loved sitting with him in his hospital room, waiting for him to wake up.

Even in his weakened and often semi-conscious condition, this saint of God taught me how to work through pain and adversity. One day he woke up while I was there and he took hold of my face, kissed my cheek and said, "Love, Joy, Peace, Love, Joy, and Peace." I knew without a doubt that he was in the presence of God. God was teaching me through this man to worship God in every adversity! He died shortly after that but his funeral was a beautiful memorial to how many people God can touch through one life totally devoted to Him. Praise Him! This godly man's example also prepared me for the next phase of my own recovery.

That lonely little girl

Restoring the Heart Ministries, which I founded in 1999, sponsors weekends of recovery for victims of childhood sexual abuse. These weekends, called Wildflower retreats, are led by facilitators who help victims get at the root issues of their woundedness. I participated in one of those retreats as part of a DVD video series we put together called "Into the Wildflowers."

Dr. Jeanette Vought, a marriage and family therapist, facilitated that particular Wildflower retreat. During a group counseling session, Jeanette asked me three piercing questions: "Julie, do you feel like the pain from your childhood is still there? What is the pain of that child? What did that little child feel?" Many feelings and thoughts began swimming in my head as I tried to answer.

Jeanette's questions brought back lots of feelings of rejection and abandonment. I had to admit that deep inside, the little girl I use to be, still didn't have a family and still really felt alone. When I have people in my life who serve as my mom, like Jeanette, it means the world to me. When I mean a mom, I mean someone who cares when I have an accident and cares that I don't die.

When I had cancer I called my parents and they didn't care. They didn't return phone calls or send me a card. Then when I had the bike accident, when I was conscious enough to speak, I called my dad and told him I almost died. I knew he didn't care. He had never seen my children, his grandchildren, so I asked him, "Would you just come out and see them?" He said, "No." And he never called back.

That little girl inside me can still feel alone. Sometimes I push people away and get real quiet, but when God gives me someone that I can let in, he shows me more of his love and acceptance that I never had at home.

My son, the bridge

In the summer of 2007 my then 19-year-old son Mathew called me on the phone from college and said, "Mom, I have a mission." I said, "What is that, honey?"

"I have a mission to love my grandparents."

The last time he saw them he was 9 years old and my father was really, really volatile and angry. So I didn't bring him in the presence of my father anymore. But Mathew said to me, "I'm supposed to go; I know God is telling me I'm supposed to save some money, buy a ticket, fly back to Montana and I'm supposed to bring the love of God to my grandparents."

So he did. I was somewhat anxious but I knew he had become a strong man both physically, emotionally and most of all spiritually and that he could take care of himself. I knew he would have to be strong in all of those areas. My parents were very angry, bitter and bigoted people.

It's very complicated to get to my parents' house. You have to fly into an airport that's four hours from them, but they came and picked him up and they were very, very good to my son. It never happened to me but it happened for my son. I was so excited.

That following summer he went to Montana for a month and worked for my father. While he was there he called and said, "Mom, I have more of the love of God that I want to bring to your parents. When I'm there, will you join me so that I can see where you went as a little girl and I can get to know that little girl in you?"

He added this very stunning comment, "I'm the bridge between your parents and you and the love of God." So I went there in May that year and saw my parents.

It's been amazing to me that God answers these deep prayers that we never even really had hope could be answered. I'd always wanted to love my parents but I didn't know how to do that because it wasn't safe to be in their proximity. It's beautiful that God would shower me with this love and answer this prayer that I had no hope of being answered. But God hopes for us when we don't even know if we can do it.

A Wildflower Thrives in Florida

What an incredible experience going back to my childhood mountains with Mathew. He wanted to know everything about my little girl years: "Mom, show me where you rode your horse"; "Mom, show me where you laid in the wildflowers"; "Show me where you used to live." Mathew took me to scene after scene of pain and we prayed over my memories. And when we were around my parents we prayed for them together. Mathew became my strength as I faced my abuse again and helped me not tremble like a leaf.

The next time I saw my parents was the summer of 2010. I was speaking in Spokane, Washington and thought I would drive to visit them since I was nearby. My mother was open to seeing me but my father was not so open. He kept avoiding seeing me; I wanted to scream!!! *I made this long trip to see you and you can't even show me the decency of giving me a little of your time*, I thought to myself in silence. *Do you realize this may be our last encounter?* I knew he was not doing well physically. But I did what I felt God called me to do: I said goodbye. My father had no emotion. In fact he acted like he was saying goodbye to some stranger.

Then early in 2011 I was at Brooklyn Tabernacle with my son Wesley and the pastor spoke of giving someone to God, someone you needed to forgive. I knew I had to give up my dad and offer him up at the cross. I had done this before but never from the depths of who I am. I cried out to God with my son's arm around my shoulders. I felt this incredible release, a great weight lifted from me. How awesome it was to have Wesley be part of that incredible experience.

A month later I was doing a film shoot in Tucson when I got a forwarded e-mail saying my father wasn't going to live through the night. I went back to the film crew, a great Christian group, and asked them to pray for my dad. "Let's pretend he is in the middle of us and let's sing hymns to him," I suggested. It was very beautiful! The odd thing is I didn't feel anything, absolutely nothing. I called my spiritual mentor and friend Dr. H. Norman Wright and asked him what this was about. He told me I should allow myself to feel

Bridges to Healing

whatever I felt. "It's OK," he assured me. "You released him as your father a long, long time ago."

My father died on a Sunday morning. I prayed to the very end that he would choose to reconcile with me—but he chose not to. As I thought about my dad, I was reminded of the Jack Nicholson/Morgan Freeman movie "The Bucket List." It's kind of a silly movie, but there's an incredible scene when Jack Nicholson's character is about to die but before that he reconciles with his daughter and grandchild. How I wish I had received that! Every little girl (and woman) longs to reconcile with her father—even after the damage of sexual and physical abuse. I didn't receive that—I pray for you who also have not received that gift; my heart goes out to you. Let us pray for one another.

With my father's death I thought the relationship with my mother would get better. Maybe she wouldn't hide the secret anymore. But it just got worse. She wouldn't return my phone calls or acknowledge the gifts and cards I sent. She wrote me a letter saying she hated me and would never forgive me for speaking badly about "her husband." It saddened me that my mother was still not able to face the reality of a husband who abused her daughter. I had to let that be my mother's choice. I couldn't force her to love me. I decided to love her in the way I could and pray for her—and let her go.

About six months after my father's death, my son Mathew and his wife Tammy told me they were expecting a baby. I was so overjoyed but also reflective. "Mathew, I know I took some courageous steps to change generations of abuse," I said. "I'm sorry if that courage has hurt you in any way. I know your inheritance has been affected—your material one—from my parents." He stopped me and said, "Mom, I know that courage was hard on you and has taken its toll, but mom, I'm so proud of you for stopping the cycle for me, my brothers and sister and our future children."

I danced inside as I heard these beautiful words!!! Was it worth the lonely nights of sobbing and saying goodbye to family to stand up for myself and my children? Yes, it was worth it, every step of the way!

Julie's 23rd Psalm

The Lord is my Father.
I'm proud to be His Daughter.
He is the Daddy I've always wanted.
He protects me from evil.
I am safe with him.
We talk all day and night.
We desire each other's presence.
Even though my mother and father have abandoned me, He has adopted me.
I am His.
I am delighted in this new relationship.
He is a father who desires to give me good things.
He pursues me with His lavish love daily.
My cup overflows!
Surely His love is never ending and we will walk hand in hand all the days of my life!

Your Time

- What messages did you receive from your mom and dad? What were the messages you learned about physical affection from your mom and dad?

- What were some of the messages that were given to you that impacted your self-identity? What messages did you receive from your siblings?

- What have you come to believe about yourself?

Chapter 12

Breaking Out

Waking up

My marriage with Matt had seen its share of turmoil. However, we had fought well through our challenges. But one challenge continued, and worsened, as our children got older.

I mentioned earlier that Matt struggled with porn use from age 12. He carried that sinful habit into our marriage and it eventually took control of him and our lives. It had come and gone over the years, but it got worse and worse during our time on the East Coast.

Those who are sexually abused often deny their emotions and the fact that they know "something is very wrong." If a sexual abuse victim becomes a wife, she may ignore warning signs in the marriage because her husband represents a security and strength that she's never known. When she becomes a mother she may deny the problems in her marriage so she can help her children grow up, be strong and thrive.

Those are the kind of decisions I made over the years. I would find a magazine and discount it as just a "man" thing, not taking seriously Jesus' message that thinking such thoughts was wrong. Instead I took his sin on myself, subconsciously blaming myself for being defective and undesirable. That's why I would catch him looking at those women on the computer; it was all me.

Rather than confront Matt's behavior, I worked harder to make myself desirable. I tried to be a beautiful woman so he wouldn't struggle with it and would only want me. My thinking was so fractured. I didn't accept that I was already a beautiful woman.

I began reading some material on marriage and also hearing messages about God's intention for marriage. My heart and mind woke up to the fact that something was wrong, but I wasn't at fault. That was a dramatic shift for me. I prayed and prayed about what was going on and began to confront Matt about his porn usage. Things didn't improve.

I was living a lie and my life and femininity began to crumble. The pornography use began to turn into violence. Not the kind of violence where he would hit me but he would trap me and put me in terror or allow my son to push me when I was sick, or threaten me when he didn't get his way. Matt's love for me was growing cold, which led him to withdraw even further. I was very vulnerable.

My husband had no strength to protect me and if I said I was afraid or tried to call out Matt would say I was making too big of a deal about it. To me it was a big deal. I began to split—in my mind. I had learned how to compartmentalize my brain, putting the pain in a big bag by the side of the road so I could get on with life. But I wasn't getting on with life. My pain was more like a ball and chain attached to both legs.

It was very challenging (and exhausting!) with my clients. I would hear their abusive experiences and think in the back of my mind, *I am going through the same thing—why can't I stand up like I am counseling them? Where do I go? I have no one to tell and does anyone even care.*

When we would have these abusive episodes my heart began to hurt and I was getting pains in my chest. I remember one incident where my chest pains took my breath away. I drove myself to the hospital; they took my blood pressure and monitored my heart. As soon as the doctors and nurses said, "We believe you; you're going to be OK, you're safe here" my heart began to pump normally and the pains went away. They kept me awhile until they knew I would go home to a safe environment.

Matt refused to take my physical symptoms seriously. He told me I was crazy. I didn't know where to turn; I was so very alone. Where do you go as the pastor's wife? If he could have heard me and stopped! I so longed to be touched by my husband again.

Unexpected response

I gathered every bit of strength I could muster and met with two elders of the church. What happened next was very painful.

The senior elder of the church proceeded to tell me that he did pornography and that his wife was fine with it. He suggested this was something I needed to accept, that a large number of pastors do pornography. Wow! I was blown away.

At the time I attended a local Catholic parish after our church service. The parish supported my ministry and I loved the holiness of the service. However, the senior elder, along with an associate pastor, told me our members were watching me and they weren't OK with it. I was told I needed to make a choice—our church or the Catholic Church. I told them I wanted to attend both but they wanted me to choose. I didn't want to pick so they said I was no longer welcome at church services. All this was done without a formal disciplinary hearing and without announcing their decision to the church.

I felt like the sacrificial lamb. All my support was gone. I had grown quite close to many in the church—they were my family! At first I would take my boys and sit in the back and slip out before the service was over so the elders couldn't see us. I felt like a crazy woman. My husband then started a sermon series on holy sexuality and my psyche began to crumble. I wasn't experiencing anything holy in our marriage; I was only experiencing the rejection of my femininity but he pretended it was all OK. I knew I had to pull my boys away—we were all so confused! They had caught him doing pornography and began to feel like Christianity was all hypocrisy.

I felt like I was that little girl again not knowing where to go; powerful men had taken over again. I was in shock and oh so lonely.

My boys and I found another church and tried to hang onto our faith. My sons were confused and hurt. They felt the church was full of hypocrites. What a nightmare! I knew I had to leave the community. People would ask me in the grocery store why they hadn't seen me in church but I felt like I had a gag order. What was I supposed to say? I knew I had no protection and if word got back to the elders the abuse I was experiencing would get worse.

The hardest decision

I prayed over and over, "God please help me—save my marriage, save me" then I felt this inner release: "Julie, save yourself not your marriage." I felt this release to let go but it was one of the hardest things I ever did. I desperately loved this man, the man I thought I had married. Why, oh why???? Why more abuse, why can't he let go of this sin that has strangled me and our marriage. I began to see these were his choices—not mine—daily choices he was making. Norman Wright helped me understand the severity of porn usage from Matthew 5:27-30, how unrepentant sin sets a dangerous precedent from Matthew 18:6-8 and what real repentance looks like from 2 Corinthians 7.

I let go and then again my world crumbled around me. All of my friends in the church turned on me as word of my decision to file for divorce got out. My girlfriends began buying Matt presents and feeling sorry for him. I got horrible e-mails, letters and dirty looks wherever I went. The message was loud and clear: the worst sin you could ever commit is divorce a pastor.

The board of my ministry was filled with people from the church and all but two left. My ministry was crumbling, my life was crumbling and worse my children were crumbling.

The next two years were filled with chaos and pain. He kept trying to convince me that he had changed but I didn't see change or transformation, I just saw denial and minimization. I felt like my life depended on his transformation. I would leave Matt for a time and stay with friends and then come back. This cycle went on over and over, round and round for two years.

I would file then I would pull back to see if things could change, then I would file again when things hadn't changed. I eagerly hoped to see transformation but I finally gave up. I kept coming back to see if it could work—maybe, maybe God will restore this marriage, maybe Matt will finally be done with the porn, maybe God will do a miracle. God became my constant, intimate companion. His presence was close like glue, never letting me go, breathing words of love and grace into me. It was an incredible spiritual experience.

God also began to bring the best people in the country around, such as my mentor Dr. H. Norman Wright, who loved me through this hurricane. They also loved my children. I was most worried about my youngest son who was in a state of confusion. He didn't know who he could trust. He and I both felt rejected by the church because when they asked me to leave he went too. He was also concerned about his mother. I tried not to cry around him but he sensed my sadness and loneliness. My second youngest son didn't know what to do with his emotions. He desperately wanted to keep our family together and tried to force me to stay. But God began to restore all of us—the ones that chose to be restored.

I learned to trust God with every ounce of energy I had left. My only treasure left was my relationship with God and my confidence that He would bring me through this. In September, 2010 I packed up our house, stored almost everything in a good friend's basement and moved to Brooklyn, NY. My 18-year-old son, the only one left at home, spent his last year in a great prep school filled with godly men that began to lead him and minister to his heart.

I picked an apartment in the middle of Brooklyn from *craigslist*. I had never even been on *craigslist* but knew exactly the apartment I was to choose and by faith I said, "Yes," not even really knowing why. However, through the months that followed, God began to show me why I should move to this apartment: I was a 5-minute walk from where my youngest son attended college; I was working at the Brooklyn Tabernacle, also only a 5-minute walk; and I was also working with churches in New York City bringing the video project I had created for the broken. Wow!!! God was so real in all of this!

Dog day

There were times of unusual testing during this period of my life. To get my mind off my troubles, I went to a very nice hotel and took a whirlpool plunge, hoping to relax. Bad move! I was allergic to something in the whirlpool and spent the whole week with really bad hives all over my body. I felt like Job; I was a mess. I couldn't sleep because I just wanted to itch, and the emotional upheaval was taking its toll.

Later in the week I was back home. I often found it healing to walk in Manhattan but this day it wasn't healing at all, but only enhanced my feeling like a worthless mess!!!! The women in Manhattan (many of them at least) look like supermodels: they are slender, very put together and apparently wealthy, wearing high heels like stilts. Their physical "perfection" intensified my sense of imperfection. "O Lord," I cried out to him, "Please, please show me that you can use me, even though I'm a broken mess." I breathed that prayer and didn't really expect God to answer it so quickly.

This lady came walking by—again, she was another Manhattan "supermodel"—and she had two little dogs on leashes. My judgmental attitude reared its ugly head. "I can't believe people put their dogs in sweaters; they don't need sweaters," I grumbled to myself. Then I noticed something imperfect amidst all this perfection—one of her little dogs had only three legs. He was hobbling along at a fast pace to keep up with his friend and he was so happy! He wagged his little tail like a windshield wiper in a thunderstorm. He even seemed to have a sweet little doggy smile. He was just happy to be alive!!! And his little doggy buddy kept looking back to make sure he could keep up. You could almost hear the other dog saying, "Catch up little friend."

Breaking Out

I was undone, right there on the street. I felt God saying to me, "I will use your brokenness! Don't let it hold you back; keep your head up; keep going (even if you only have 3 legs). Keep smiling my Beloved Daughter." I laughed and cried at the same time as I delighted in these little doggies that God put in my path. I wanted to grab their cute little faces and kiss their ears. I was so happy for my little broken dog friend. He had found a companion who didn't judge him in his brokenness, who didn't bark at him and start a dogfight because he didn't measure up. God gave me incredible joy in the middle of my sobs and laughter.

Two days later it was my birthday. I got tons of comments on *Facebook* and e-mails from people all over the country who went through the Wildflowers program. The Lord reminded me of the healing He is doing in others' lives from my own pain and brokenness. It is over-the-top beautiful. Thank you God for encouraging my broken heart! I love you so!!

This all occurred about Christmas time and God brought me new understanding of Mary, the mother of Jesus. In the Scriptures there is no mention of Mary's moral worthiness, preparedness or achievement. She was just a humble servant that said, "Yes!" She wasn't trying to manage God, manufacture her own worthiness or perform for His acceptance. She didn't try to fix or control. I pray that, instead of simmering in my own damaging self-assessments, I will just say "Yes" to Jesus. Whatever you have for me, whoever you put in my path, I pray I will let go of earning your love, performing for you or attempting to be perfect and trust that who I am in You is enough.

Your Time

- In what ways have you learned who you really are? Are you able to come up with 3 things that are special about you?
- What hinders you from openly sharing your feelings and dealing honestly with yourself?
- What do you think would happen if you started coming to

A Wildflower Thrives in Florida

terms with how others were responsible for bad things happening to you? Does that make you nervous or scared? Can you let that fear go and ask God to help you move forward toward healing today?

Chapter 13

Crushed but Not Destroyed

A friend indeed

I SPENT A LOT of time healing—healing from a broken marriage, a broken heart, and broken femininity. I felt like a wildflower almost completely broken at the stem. But this broken flower held on; the spirit of God was alive and very well within me, supplying nourishment through the roots and replenishing my heart and soul.

I met some wonderful, wonderful people during this time too, people who brought God's love to me in miraculous ways. Christopher West, the best-selling author and speaker about love and sexuality, became an agent of deep restoration. I believe he listened to God and told me what God wanted me to hear. He was a witness of God for me and other women I counsel who need their beauty restored.

I contacted Christopher after listening to one of his tapes on femininity. I knew we had to have him in our Wildflower series on femininity. When I met him I felt like I'd met my brother. He began to show and tell me how very special I was as a woman and that I was chosen to speak to other women about their own blessedness. He spoke passionately about the beauty of women.

During the filming of the series I shared that I grew up in western Montana. His children are homeschooled and his wife Wendy was teaching them about the American Indians who lived in Montana. I asked them if they wanted to go to western Montana and see what they were studying, so we did: Christopher, his two sons, Christopher's publisher Matt Pinto, two of Matt's boys, my sons JonMichael, Wesley and Mathew, Mathew's wife Tammy, and me. We took horses way up into the Rocky Mountains and Christopher helped me understand that I was worth the trip. He said amazing prayers for me about the wounding of my feminine heart and the sexual abuse I had endured; it was incredible. I truly believe God brought Christopher into my life to help restore my own heart and the hearts of many, many others.

Since then we have done events together and he spoke at the Restoring the Heart fashion show in 2011. I love introducing Christopher and his writings to women so they can see how to restore their femininity and sexuality. He is a great friend. When something is really important I call and ask him for prayer.

Subway encounter

After the divorce God's healing also came to me as I loved others. I saw God's strength flow through me as I loved and ministered to the broken in the subways and on the street. God and his spirit loved my heart as He led me exactly to those I was to love with His love.

I had just finished leading a group of women through John Eldredge's book, *Walking with God*. I was especially tuned in to John's message of following the Spirit and how God uses the broken heart to keep us grounded in our need for Him as the ultimate answer to desire. My own broken heart told me how true that was. So as I stepped on the subway, John's words were hovering in the air: "I can let my disappointments define my life. Or I can let them take me back to God, to find my life in him in ways I have not yet learned."[7]

These words were never truer than the night I met Rita and Joseph. These beautiful people looked so grieved as they sat on the subway. I had to choose—excuse myself as too hurting to do them any good or move with the Spirit's nudging. I sat down next to them and asked if I could help. "I've just lost my three 3 children in a car accident," Joseph said. "They were 19, 16 and 14. My wife is just coming out of a coma and we are going to tell her tomorrow that our children are all gone." How devastating.

I offered to go with them when they spoke to her and they agreed. I had bought myself a dozen white roses, something to brighten my own day, but God meant the roses for these two very sad people. I handed them to Rita as I hopped off the subway; she burst into tears as I said goodbye.

As I walked home I mourned for my heartbroken subway companions Rita and Joseph. My spirit groaned with sorrowful cries and prayers for these people. I pled and prayed, pined and hoped their pain would be carried to Jesus. I couldn't stop thinking of the words Rita shared with me over and over: "God bringeth and taketh away; I don't understand." I was aware that I have no words, no wisdom, only the love of God. I remembered the psalmist as I lifted them to My King: "My soul yearns, even faints, for the courts of the Lord; my heart and my flesh cry out for the living God." (Ps. 84:2, NIV)

Out of my despair, and the despair of people like Rita and Joseph, I realized that cut-flower prayers no longer satisfied my soul. Cordial and modest prayers were too meek. From this experience I committed to go deeper in my desire for God in prayer, to pray with abandon for this hurting world. I was convicted through these grief-stricken people about my own superficial prayers for my petty problems in this life.

While Jesus was here on earth "he offered prayers and pleadings, with a loud cry and tears" (Hebrews 5:7, NLT). My heart went to a place of sorrowful cries for the world. "Please Lord, Abba Father, bring your love to this hurting world," I prayed. "Our souls are in anguish for one another. Please, wherever we are, introduce us to people that so desperately need you! My heart hungers for more of you for my sweet brothers and sisters."

As I have learned to pour my heart out in reckless faith, he affirms me that I am only His—beautiful and treasured—and that He will restore my heart. God is giving me the heart to fight. I am more than what is hurting me; all the lies that I held inside so long are nothing in the shadow of the cross. I am made for so much more than all of this. Long before the world began he chose me to reach out to the hurting wherever I am and meet them in their abuse, their pain, their trauma. How honored I am that he chose me!

Reckless Abandonment

Yes, my Beloved you have had a busted heart —
  A busted life —
  But now hold onto me
  You are to start a revolution, a love revolution
  Simply show the world the Love I have given you
  Give it all you have—my love is how you live, where you reside—I am your home!
  My love is what keeps your passions alive —
  Simply Listen to me-the lover of your Soul-listen and obey
  Obey with reckless abandonment
  Sing Alleluia as you remember your trauma—sing alleluia as it floods your memories, because
  As you recall and sing alleluia you will call others to remember me in their memories of atrocities —
  Voice the unvoiceable, speak the unspeakable, articulate what has been locked away, and as you do you will become part of The Bigger story to many all over the world as your pain and trauma meets others and your joy in your Father enters into their pain and trauma. You my Beloved are part of a bigger
  Story! This is much bigger than you—much bigger than your chaos; I am creating something heavenly in you as you share it with a world of unspeakable pain.
  I am in your pain, I am in your breath, I am in your sight, I am in your dreams, and I am in the voice that sings to you at night—as you sing back
  Now sing back-loud! Sing back extravagantly

God has made you uniquely for his purposes in such a time as this. He has gifted you specially and uniquely to carry this cross of love for the world.

I have not forgotten you, as you allow me I will care for your deep trauma—I will give you people that love and listen to me who can handle it and love you through it tenderly—just receive what I am giving you through them. Just let go and speak out and feel the trauma as I enter into the deepest part of the darkness. I will give you everything you need, mountains of love, I will be with you in each and every encounter—you you you are my Beloved. The fire of my passionate love resides in you!

I am designing something heavenly in you, in your soul will reside a volcano of love and healing for you and the world.

Your Time:

- Did you know to the core of your being that you were loved, special, worth protecting and delighted in? I pray so. But I know that for many of us the life we had as a child was a far cry from healthy. Do you grieve your relationship with your father? Your mother? How does that grief feel? Emotionally? Physically? Spiritually? Sexually?
- Do you have people to help you "fight the good fight" of recovering from trauma?
- What steps are you going to take to bring healing to yourself? How will you begin to give to others as part of your own healing?
- How do you access the heart of God? Do you experience His tenderness of love? Strength of love?

Chapter 14

A (Birthday) Candle in the Dark

Strange phone call

I'VE LEARNED THAT GOD'S movement in my life is never ever boring! He is such a wonderful, surprising Father. He taught me that lesson again after I received awards from New York state and federal legislators for my trauma work.

"You want to come and meet with the girls in the club," the man's voice on the phone asked. He'd seen the stories about me in the local newspapers. "A lot of my employees have been traumatized," he added. I was curious about the kind of "club" he owned, so I got on the Internet as I spoke with him. The images that popped up on my computer screen made me gasp; this man's "employees" were strippers.

I wasn't sure about visiting the club, located on Long Island where I lived at the time. But God was telling me to go! I walked through the club doors and was so completely shocked and saddened. How could these girls live this way without anyone to love them? I was so incredibly grieved, especially as I realized no one was reaching out to these lost, beautiful women.

I hurried to the restroom to give my mind and heart a moment to take all this in. But there was one more surprise: the women's bathroom doubled as the girls' dressing and undressing area. There they were, in various levels of nakedness, talking, looking in mirrors, showing off and getting ready for the next show. I was flustered and so very confused. "Lord, show me what to do here," I called out from my heart. Then I overheard two dancers talking. "It's my birthday today," said one girl. "No one remembers my birthday anymore." I knew God was giving me a message.

My friend Eric, who has Asperger's syndrome, was working in the club doing holiday drawings on windows and mirrors. Eric is probably the only man who could be in such a place without being tempted. He has an uncanny ability, because of his condition, to focus on just one thing and for him that's his artwork.

I grabbed Eric and said, "We're on a mission! We need the biggest birthday cake we can find." The only thing I could find was an ice cream cake that served a hundred people. It was summer and the club was packed, even though it was a weekday night. The birthday girl was dancing and I waited till she finished. "Excuse me," I said, approaching her. "God knows it's your birthday and you're not forgotten." She burst into tears.

Another dancer came up and commented, "It was my birthday yesterday and no one remembered." Then the two girls hugged each other and sobbed. It was a touching, wonderful moment in such a dark place. These clubs are filled with young girls and customers often pay for illegal sexual contact.

Then the DJ cued up the "Happy Birthday Song" and everyone in the club began singing their hearts out—the girls, the bouncers, the bartenders and customers. We cut up the cake, which was beginning to melt by then, and Eric handed it out to everyone. I couldn't have imagined this scene, with all its humor, sadness and blessing.

From then on I determined to go into the club once a month with a birthday cake for these forgotten daughters. "It's Angel's birthday this month, she likes carrot cake," the club owner would tell me. The birthday party became this incredible event and the girls were so excited when I came in. I was the birthday party lady!

After a while I would go into the club even if it wasn't birthday time. One time Eric told me there was a masquerade party for Halloween. I came dressed up as a blue mermaid, with a funny wig and fake eyelashes, a sequin dress and fins. But Eric had the date wrong! I felt so stupid and out of place. I started thinking, *Why am I such an idiot God; I'm the only one dressed up.*

Then a girl who'd been dancing sat next to me and began pouring out her story. She told me she planned to commit suicide that night. We talked and talked, for two straight hours. As the hour approached eleven, I knew it was time to go. The club was always a dark place but it became even more violent and dangerous as it got closer to midnight. But as we got up to leave, this despairing girl said, "I'm going to live now." And she did.

During our conversation this young woman told me a dream she'd had a few days before. She was in the club, performing, and it was very dark, more dark than normal. Then, very suddenly, the doors opened and light poured into the room. A man became visible; it was Jesus. He then walked into the club and carried each girl out. "He sent you in here, didn't he?" she asked.

This wasn't the only time I heard about this dream. At least three of the girls had the same dream, at different times, and told me about it. This was so phenomenal to me, that God had chosen to use me in the lives of these girls. Oh thank you so much Jesus!

I continued taking birthday cakes into that club, and other clubs, for several years. Many caring Christian people were afraid for me, but I needed to love these girls and the others who worked there. God filled my heart with his compassion every time I poured myself into these hurting people.

Even the rough and tough bouncers would say, "Hey, it's my birthday!" It was funny and touching hearing a strong, fearsome man asking for birthday cake. I'd ask them who remembered their birthdays in the past and about favorite birthdays growing up. Customers would respond to my questions too and I could see for a moment the little boy each man use to be. Childhood stories would tumble out. I began looking at them and thinking, "They're just like all of us, all desperately seeking love."

Then in 2010 I organized the first Restoring the Heart fashion show. Girls from the clubs and women who'd been through Wildflowers retreats graced the runway as fashion models. Everyone in the room was stunned at what happened there. I noticed people weeping as they saw the beauty of these girls. I would so love to bring this fashion show all over the United States, because these clubs are everywhere, and these girls need us to reach out and help them.

After that 2010 show, one of the club girls called me the next day saying she decided to leave the business. "For the first time in my life I didn't have to do drugs or alcohol to have a good time," she said. "Last night I just wanted to feel every drop of love in that room. And I know it had something to do with God."

Ten of the girls I met in the clubs decided to leave the business. A number of them accepted Christ. Sadly, it was difficult finding churches that accepted the girls, although we did eventually find places for these rescued daughters to know Jesus more deeply. In fact, only one church ever financially supported the fashion show, although the event was respectable and first class all the way. That disappointed me but it did not deter me from continuing to help these young women toward a loving Father who does not exploit, but cherishes and protects.

I've had a number of people ask me if I was afraid going in the clubs. I was a little fearful at first but that went away quickly. When you feel the love of God you become bold. He protected me as I went. That doesn't mean there aren't shocking things going on in these places. I needed prayer when I visited the clubs, prayers of protection covering me on all sides. I also needed people who could listen and let me process my experiences. But the clubs aren't scary anymore because the Lord is my protector. I don't feel those fears anymore.

Your Time:

- God has restored me and strengthened me to the point I can go into places that are scary for many others, like strip clubs. This has taken me many years and the healing power of Jesus ministered through many caring people. As you begin to heal, where do you hope you might be able to go to help others?
- Many of the young women in the clubs have believed lies about their sexuality. Have you believed lies about your sexuality?

What are the lies? If you don't know can you pray that God will show you?

- Who has been an instrument of healing in your life? How have they loved you well?

CHAPTER 15

Embracing Trauma Far Away

Africa

TRAUMA KNOWS NO BOUNDARIES, sadly. Everywhere I've traveled in the U.S. I've met hurting people who weren't sure which way was up or how they'd ever come back from the sadness and loss they'd experienced. I've been there myself. It's awful.

But over the last few years I'd heard about the atrocities committed in Uganda, Sudan, the Central African Republic and the Democratic Republic of the Congo by a man named Joseph Kony and his Lord's Resistance Army (LRA). Young children abducted from their families in the middle of the night. Boys forced to kill their parents as part of their "induction" into Kony's army; girls given as sex slaves to his officers. Kony has had dozens of "wives" himself. It made me sick to think about the gross disrespect for childhood and for life.

In December, 2011, I was asked as part of a trauma team to bring the Wildflowers project to Uganda. African Leadership and Reconciliation Ministries (ALARM) invited us to train 50 mentors working with children who escaped the LRA.

In July 2012, we traveled to Gulu, Uganda. We taught these mentors how to help these children heal from their profound psychological and spiritual wounds. The mentors themselves came out of Kony's clutches and needed our love and attention. These young people have been so horribly traumatized, and have been the agents of trauma as well. They needed the specialized kind of counseling we were able to offer, and our hope is that many more Christian counseling professionals will follow. They need this time of healing to have any chance of returning to their home villages.

I observed how the mentors interacted with the children, which provided insight to share with them about how to help these traumatized little ones. What a privilege to let these children know they're loved, that God loves them and someone wants to hear their stories. Kony claims to know God but he teaches lies about God that promote his cruel and twisted agenda. To offer them the hope of transformation, based on who God really is and how He's changed me, was such an awesome experience.

My hope is that this first effort in Uganda will spread within that country and beyond its borders. I don't want this to be the only time I visit Uganda, but want to keep bringing the message of hope Jesus offers. To hear the children's stories, to really bring the truth of what they've been through into the light of God's kindness, this is our strong desire. With God's help we will be resilient enough to handle anything that comes at us.

I've not worried about the danger of going to a place like Gulu, because this is what God created me to do. The Lord made me for such a time as this; He created in me a program to help myself and these children who are so traumatized. I'm at a place where I can handle my own story but also handle other stories and love others through their story.

The more I connect with the Holy Spirit, the more courage he gives me. I'm not afraid of trauma but I want to run towards the people who've been traumatized, whether that's in New York City, Florida or Uganda. It's very lonely when you've been so traumatized and I want to be with them through their emotional and spiritual recovery.

The children of Gulu need more than someone to say, "Forget the past; move on." I've encountered that in the church and it doesn't help the broken heart. I want to create a safe space for them to grieve and express their anger—to let them be human! There will be a time for singing songs and sharing Scripture, but they need this soul space first, and that's what God has created in me to provide. Because of my abuse, I have drunk in every ounce of healing the Lord has offered. People like me are the ones who can be wounded healers to children like this.

Your Time:

- How are the tentacles of the past being released from you?
- What do you feel the Lord is calling you to focus on now? Your marriage, parenting, relationships?
- How is the Lord calling you to move into the lives of other people with what you have learned?
- How has this healing process affected your dignity?

Chapter 16

Interrupted but Restored

Grace flood

IN THE FIRST CHAPTER of Genesis God tells us that he made people in his image. "So God created man in his own image, in the image of God he created him; male and female he created them. God blessed them and said to them, 'Be fruitful and increase in number; fill the earth and subdue it. Rule over the fish of the sea and the birds of the air and over every living creature that moves on the ground.'" (Genesis 1:27-28, NIV)

Sin interrupted this wonderful plan God had for man and woman to care for each other and watch over the earth together. Trauma upsets the apple cart even further. What remains of the image of God in us is shattered and left in a jumble on the ground.

To sum up in a few paragraphs what God has done in my life is impossible. My heart is bursting with thankfulness. He is the father I've always wanted. He is indeed my "sacred romance" as he pursues me with his love daily.

In Psalm 27:10 it says, "Though my father and mother forsake me, the Lord will receive me" (NIV). God has done that in my life in a marvelous way. He desires to give you this joy as He restores your life and makes you a source of restoration for others.

Sue Monk Kidd writes: "I'm discovering that a spiritual journey is a lot like a poem. You don't merely recite a poem or analyze it intellectually. You dance it, sing it, cry it and feel it on your skin and in your bones. You move with it and feel its caress. It falls on you like a teardrop or wraps around you like a smile. It lives in the heart and the body as well as the spirit and the head."[8]

In the center of our mourning and grief, we are reminded of our smallness. For in our smallness, Jesus invites us to rise up and dance. For in our suffering (not apart from it) the promise of Psalm 30:11 becomes a reality: "You have turned my mourning into dancing" (NASB). As Henri Nouwen says, "At the center of our grief we find the grace of God."[9]

Love applied

Today I feel as though God has flooded my life with grace:

- His love was applied to me in the middle of the Rocky Mountains as a little girl on my horse Chico.
- His love was applied to me in the middle of my sexual/physical/mental abuse (as I look back he showed himself to me even there).
- His love was applied to me in my waywardness with promiscuity/drugs/alcohol when He drew me back to Him as my Father.
- His loved applied to me in forgiving myself after my abortions and applying God's love to others.
- His love applied to me in instructing me how to mother well (when I didn't have a clue).
- His love applied to me in the middle of my cancer, and in my bike accident that caused a brain injury.
- And now God's love is applied to me in the middle of every single minute of the day as I travel and meet amazing people all over the country. His love is bursting within me and out of me. I feel like a limitless fountain of overflowing love.

A Wildflower Thrives in Florida

I work as ministry outreach representative for Timberline Knolls (TK), a residential treatment center in Chicago, setting up Wildflower groups all over the country to teach people how they can love one another as God loves them. I had been referring many people to TK through my work with the Wildflowers Project and I am so thrilled now to work with them. They do such a great job with women and girls struggling with eating disorders, addiction, mood disorders, trauma and co-occurring disorders.

The unique approach of TK and their individualized programming meets each woman's needs by building upon her own strength and potential. They have a great ministry track where miracles unfold life after glorious life.

In addition to my work with TK, I have been asked, along with Linda Cochrane of CareNet, to serve as a co-chair for one of the American Association of Christian Counselors' new member divisions. The *Crisis Pregnancy and Abortion Recovery Network* seeks to train and equip Christian counselors, pastors, and caregivers to offer competent counsel and soul care to individuals and couples facing an unplanned pregnancy or struggling in the wake of an abortion.

I'm also very excited about the chance to work with Recovery Associates (RA). They provide an alternative to traditional 30-day lockdown substance abuse treatment in south Florida. Bill Peevy, RA care consultant, is a wonderful man who has his own amazing story of recovery through the grace of Jesus. He says that only six to ten percent of addicts and alcoholics will stay off drugs after intensive rehabilitation, mainly because they don't get to apply what they're learning in real life.

RA interacts with a network of transitional living facilities where recovery can continue for many months in a monitored environment after the 30 days. As Bill can testify, many of those with substance-abuse issues also have experienced sexual abuse, both men and women. The process of untangling the truth from the lies takes time. It also takes an environment where facility managers can keep track of patients' behavior. It's a lot easier to pretend everything's OK with a therapist you're only seeing once a month than with people who know how you've been living 24/7. I very much look forward to working with RA, especially in adapting the Wildflower curriculum for men.

Through my work with TK, the Wildflower Project, AACC and Recovery Associates, I'm learning to live my life wide open. But I know many who fear such an open-handed approach to God or anyone else. They possess no passion for pursuing their desires. Their hearts have been muted by the assaults they've endured. Please allow God to capture your heart again! He wants to romance you with his tender spirit! Love makes recovery and joy possible—let's not miss a drop that God has to offer us. Let's offer a collaborative voice of love for one another as we unwrap our deep-down passions, cravings and desires.

Let's all live our lives with wide open hearts! "Whatever you do, do it heartily, as to the Lord and not to men" (Colossians 3:23, NKJV). This passion is sustainable—wide open, over the top, ready to bless the world around us with the blessings and extravagant love we have received. Let us dare to be excited again to live our dreams and be catapulted into the adventure of extraordinary living. It's living out loud, learning to be fully human and fully alive!

Who Am I?

I am a Wildflower
I am a Tapestry
Threads woven in pain
Cords of joy
I am a masterpiece;
Of once abuse and pain, but now
Passion, joy and extravagant love
I am artistic pain,
Flung out now to love the world with the
Love of God
I am a live montage
Of courage, resilience, receiving every
Drop of mercy my Savior bestows upon me.

A Wildflower Thrives in Florida

A study in still life,
Once colored unclean, now brought to
Seeing her God with a hopeful, pure and generous heart.
The brushstrokes of God become more and more
Bold with the overwhelming depth of the love of God
Etched deeply into who I am
—a woman, ragged, torn physically,
Sexually, emotionally but now bursting
Forth into a foreign world with a feminine warrior heart
And the shield of God surrounding me—the banner of love over me,
Passion, incredible joy—this wildflower has become a wild rose
With many thorns but now bursting forth with the sweet scent of the love of God . . .

Your Time:

- Are you willing to be a healing presence in another's life? If so, who needs your healing presence right now? What is one practical way that you can be a "wounded healer" to others? (Please be specific.)
- As you begin living life with an open, passionate heart, how will you continue drawing from God's heart? How will you let him be your shield and your protector? How will you continue to let others know you and love you well?
- What does the future look like to you right now? Share your ideas by writing in your journal or by drawing pictures that represent that future.

CHAPTER 17

A Wildflower Continues Her Adventures

My nightmare

Do you ever wake up and feel like you've walked into your story (scene 2) not knowing how you got here or where your headed? The first scene of my story was riddled with pain, sorrow, and a whole lot of tragedy. As I enter the next scene I pray, "Lord, what is this all about; how do I pray?" As I look around I really don't know what God is up to. I do, but I don't—I know he is up to giving me a BIG BEAUTIFUL LIFE. I have been at the end of the road many times. How God could create a miracle out of the nothing of me renders me speechless. Every earthly option is exhausted. I keep reaching out to hope beyond this little limited life. I admit, at times I have just jumped in and started praying my little pathetic prayer speeches to God. It felt like it hit dead air. I was randomly swinging the sword around in the air. I felt like I blew it, that prayer doesn't really work, and that God had given up on me. How wrong I was! John says, "This is confidence we have in approaching God; that if we ask anything according to his will, he hears us. And if we know that he hears us-whatever we ask-we know that we have what we asked of him" (1 John 5:14–15).

There it is! The awesome promise of answered prayer. If we pray according to God's will, he hears and answers! And if we don't know what to pray, we simply ask. This has totally revolutionized the way I pray—and WOW! Just as Scripture promised I am seeing fruits of answered prayer. I count every blessing!

I want to be one of those like the saints of yesterday and today that spark a revolution. I commit to "going all in" not living partial obedience but kneeling in prayer for a submitted life. A few nights ago I was with a delightful group of Christian new friends. A man asked a good question.

When life falls apart what is the first thing you do? Out of a group of thirty only two of us answered that we desperately go to God. The rest tried to figure everything out first before going to God. Maybe I have made just too much of mess of things—I desperately HAVE to go to God first. I passionately want to view culture through the word of God. The authoritative, infallible word of God. Otherwise I wreck myself. "So do not throw away this confident trust in the Lord. Remember the great reward it brings you! Patient endurance is what you need now, so that you will continue took do God's will. Then you will receive all that he has promised" (Hebrews 10:35–36). I HAVE to make a deliberate determination to give God authority over my life, otherwise I automatically drift when distractions come. And believe me our whole life is filled with distractions that bring us to partial obedience. There is no such thing as partial obedience.

So today God is giving me a vision of truth. He is asking me to recall the moment where I was saved. When he spoke to me with a heart of love the night I tried to commit suicide. His love touched me as he saved my life. He brought me a new proposal and I said yes! "Choose for yourselves this day whom you will serve." This proposal was between me and God—do not "confer with flesh and blood" (Galatians 1:16). All I know is that God is my only hope. He turns my heart to him as he constantly is wooing me! He kindly wins back my affections as I turn my heart back to him. God is our divine spouse, always taking the intuitive. So how do I pray today? I merely ask God. Oh Lord, I need you.

It may appear that I have been silent in the years since I wrote the first version of *A Wildflower Grows in Brooklyn*, but those silent years weren't silent, externally or internally. During that time God used so many people in my life to love me, help me move, and be my New York family. I knew I would greatly miss them but I also knew God had closed this door and was opening a big one in Florida. The year was 2013; I was ready to move on. The step I took was a bit radical. I packed up all that I had in my Brooklyn apartment and bought a house 1,200 miles away. I moved to a place where I knew no one. Why? I wasn't sure. I hadn't worked out all the details. Because my job at the time involved a lot of traveling, I was free to live anywhere. Why not Florida?! It seemed full of opportunities. My rent was high in Brooklyn and it kept going up and up and up. I had been living there with my youngest son, Wesley. He had gone to college in downtown Brooklyn at St. Francis College but had recently moved to Chicago to go to North Park University where he was offered a great soccer scholarship. So I had no reason to stay. I bought a cute little house close to the beach for one-fifth of what I was paying for that two-bedroom apartment on Gold Street in Brooklyn.

I packed up my stuff and my dreams because I knew God had a plan. This little house became my own sweet sanctuary, a place where God and I communicated and loved one another to the depths of who I am. It was a glorious respite. My little sanctuary had three bedrooms (one I used for my office). It was in a townhome complex and I had a little corner lot that adjoined a golf course. I lived only a few miles from the beach and so enjoyed my nightly walks praying and listening to the waves crash against the shore.

And so began my three-year journey in south Florida, home to more treatment centers than anywhere else in the world. (There are 170 treatment centers in West Palm Beach.) God led me into an incredible work of bringing the addicted to Christ and working through their trauma wounds. I took them through the Wildflower and Into My Arms curriculum to help them heal from their sexual abuse and postabortive wounds. I trained the Christian staff at some of these treatment centers how to work with the trauma of childhood sexual abuse and postabortion.

A Wildflower Thrives in Florida

I would also go and speak to the residents. I would sit in the middle surrounded by sometimes up to eighty residents, share my story of addiction and abuse, and then open it up for prayer. It was absolutely mind-blowingly miraculous watching the addicted invite Jesus into their lives! Interestingly enough, I worked with men the most in these treatment centers—men who had been sexually abused and who struggled with their sexual identity and others who had been in the military and were suffering from trauma. I was so blessed and honored to work with these very vulnerable people who were holding onto their lives by a thread.

As I did ministry, I also began to date a few men, but I tried to be selective. One day I met a man named Paul at a Christian treatment conference. Right from the beginning it felt like we had an amazing connection. He appeared to be a strong Christian and was very good looking. He pursued me right from the start—he seemed to have a purpose of winning my heart. What an incredible gift from God! Or so I thought.

I'll confess, even after all I'd been through, my thinking was still flawed. Deep down, I felt that I was incomplete as a single person and that I needed to be completed by a man. I was struggling with this inner conflict as well as a sense of loneliness. The enemy used this loneliness to fuel anxiety, and this anxiety said to me, "You must find a man to soothe this loneliness"

As you read this story about my short, abusive marriage (it lasted only forty-four days) and the stories of other women in similar abusive marriages, please know that there are thousands of women who are sharing the same nightmare. Yes, I married a nightmare and I was living a nightmare. My question for you all is, how do you deal with a nightmare? I know it's risky to put my nightmare relationship out there, but please know that in my speaking the truth of this nightmare I find healing and pray you will find healing in your nightmare too. There is an alternative! God will teach you to stand up strong and walk away, if that is what he is leading you to do. He will help you gather up all of the strength you can muster as you walk in His strength. I remember the day I left Paul I had to use all of the self-talk I could find. I said

A Wildflower Continues Her Adventures

to myself, "You are strong enough, you can do this! Jesus please help me" over and over again as I shook like a leaf.

Prior to going on a second date, I had asked Paul to undergo psychological testing. I knew it seemed like a strange request, but I really had come to a place of mistrust toward men and needed assurance that he was healthy. After he underwent testing, he would not reveal the results to me. This was a huge red flag. But I ignored this warning and continued seeing him. Soon he began pushing for marriage. At this point, I asked him to meet my friends. I knew I needed their discernment. He spent over two hours with my friend Sharon and her husband Jim, and they asked him an abundance of personal questions. I knew they would be out for my best interest. They felt like I should continue on with this relationship. I look back now and see what a classic, narcissistic con man he was—he could con the best of them by giving the answers that he knew would satisfy. He knew it and would later say with pride that he was the master imposter; no one would see who he really was. He was indeed clever and deceptive. He had been down this path before, but I was deceived. He had multiple personalities and they emerged at different times and in different places. I was thrown off balance and couldn't figure out who I was dealing with.

I recall a client I had years ago. Susan's husband Don was a multiple. One of his personalities was obsessed with details. Because Susan was a strong Christian and was committed to remaining pure before marriage, she didn't spend a lot of time alone with Don—she didn't want to be tempted sexually and didn't want to give him the temptation. But when she moved into his home she was amazed at the detail of everything in place. The towels were all just right and hung perfectly. The labels of cans and items in the pantry all perfectly facing the front. If he saw something off (maybe a picture or a piece of furniture not in perfect alignment) he would get rather cranky until it was all lined up.

Even with clothing, if there was a small spot on anything you couldn't wear it and had to throw it away. He was indeed meticulous. She remembers helping him with little things like picking up his dry cleaning. She had to bring the receipt to pick it up and also deliver the receipt back to him, signifying that she had picked it up or dropped it off. All these rules made her head spin, and especially if she didn't keep all the rules in exact order. As he had said many times, if she didn't learn to think like him and do all his routines correctly, he would make her life hell, but then he would quickly switch personalities and be charming, kind and tender. She never knew who she was dealing with!

As I reflected on the similarity between her relationship with Don and mine with Paul, I began to ask myself, why? Why didn't I see what the future would hold for me if we married? This was not normal. It was a nightmare out of a Hollywood movie.

I am not the only woman who has lived this nightmare. I think of Margie. Margie was raised in a good Christian home. She had just come out of an abusive marriage to Ron. Ron and Margie had two boys, and Margie came in one day and discovered Ron sexually abusing her three-year-old son, so she mustered up all the strength she could find and left, moving herself and her two sons in with her parents. One night she went to a bar with a girlfriend. In comes Mike, who "swept her off her feet." Charming, gregarious, handsome—he had it all! He came in with cowboy boots, a gun on his hip, and a ten gallon hat. As he approached Margie, he said, "You're just the cutest thing I've ever laid my eyes on." He had her right there! She introduced him to her parents, who were quite taken by him. He was her savior, a new father for her and her sons! A man who truly loved her (or so she thought). He quickly put a big diamond ring on her finger. She was thrilled!

But on her honeymoon she became concerned. He seemed to watch her every move. If she was away from him for more than a few minutes, he would start accusing her of finding another man. He was insanely jealous. When they came home from the honeymoon, he was relentless in making sure she connected with him every thirty to forty minutes. It was very hard to work. If she had a project that needed concentrated time, he would become livid at her for not texting or calling him all day. Her life became a nightmare. Margie's sister Barbara became concerned and wanted to take Margie away on a girls vacation. Margie begged Mike to let her go, and finally after months of begging, he let her. But only with the stipulation that she connect with him via text or phone all day. She agreed and happily went to a beautiful beach hotel with her sister. So all day, every half-hour Mike was texting her. If she didn't answer right away he would be accusing her of having an affair, or flirting with other men. The second night she went to a restaurant about a half-hour away from the hotel. Margie made a HUGE mistake—she left her phone at the hotel. She had a great time with her sister but when she got to the hotel and turned on her phone she, knew she was in BIG trouble! He had called her over twenty times, swearing at her, accusing her of being a "whore." Within one hour after begging in the hotel he showed up—ten gallon hat, gun on his hip, face red as could be, pounding on the hotel door. Barbara didn't know what to do to protect her sister. Barbara asked her sister to come in the other room for a few minutes and tried to talk to her into staying. Margie knew she couldn't—that would only make things worse.

This event was over fifteen years ago. Margie is still with Mike. She knows deep down she should walk out of this nightmare, which of course has gotten even worse, but she doesn't want to disappoint God and other Christians by having a second divorce.

Paul called me day and night and had an unrelenting obsession with where I was, who I was with, and what I was doing. The nightmare continued and intensified. He was exhausting. And I thought it so strange that he always wore a formal suit to work. I mean, come on, this is Florida! You're in the hot sun working in a treatment center. The other men wore nice casual clothes but now as I look back, this was his obsession with perfectionism. He always had to look the part and now I did too. If I was to be seen in church with him, I had to dress perfectly. We had to look like the "model couple." His church and personal life were so disconnected I never ever knew who I was dealing with.

He became part of my ministry—Restoring the Heart. He was obsessed with financial details. I remember my bookkeeper being on the phone with him. He pushed her so hard she started to cry. This made me furious. It was one thing to push me to the limit but not Sally—don't you hurt her! I demanded that he apologize. He got on the phone and said in a fake sweet voice, "Oh Sally, sweetheart, I'm sorry you're so sensitive but you have to do things right." He got off the phone and called her a dumb bitch. Why, oh, why didn't I see this sickness and leave? He then took me out and bought me a lovely dinner. As I look back on this relationship I see that since my father was a psychopath, I had learned as a young girl to adapt myself to psychopathic behavior.

Yes, I was concerned about his obsessions, his pushiness, the way he bullied people, the way he obsessed about little details until he drove us both crazy, his critical comments about me (for which he would apologize and then bring me a dozen roses), his aggression, his total lack of compassion, his over-the-top entitlement. As I reflect back on this time, I'm amazed that after so many years, I still could be blinded by the lie that a man could love in the place that only God could.

Sadly, I shut out the voice of truth in the Holy Spirit. Within two months of meeting Paul, we were engaged. He bought me a beautiful ring. I fell in love with his kind, welcoming family. Finally I had a family! I especially loved the way his father loved his step-mother (his mother had died five years before I met him). I guess I thought that would happen for me as well.

The afternoon he asked me to marry him I had received a cruel letter from my own mother saying that she never wanted to hear from me again and that she was disowning me as her daughter. She had expressed this before, but seeing it in a letter was devastating. I felt crushed and my sense of loneliness was activated again. The promise of a family (Paul's family) regardless of the cost became an even more seductive temptation. My newfound beau rode in and rescued me, asking him to marry him. I said, "Yes!" with great excitement. Finally, a family that loved me. This bittersweet hope still beguiled me.

As soon as we became engaged Paul made an appointment with his lawyer. Paul was adamant that I sign over my house and car to him as well as my finances. It was his own lawyer that confronted him and said, "Slow down, Paul. You still have months before you marry. Why the hurry?" Needless to say, Paul was angry at his attorney. Two weeks before the wedding Paul brought me to his lawyer once more, demanding that I put him on my retirement fund with my work, put him on my will, and sign over my house and car to him. Once again, the lawyer told him to slow down, since we could do all of this paperwork AFTER we were married, when we returned from the honeymoon. Paul laughed that crazy, evil laugh that I had become terrified of. He actually said, "What if she drowns on vacation—we're going to an island you know." I shared about these lawyer appointments with my friend Richard, who became very concerned about me marrying Paul. These appointments with Paul's lawyer put Richard on high alert and he said, "Julie, you can walk away." He pleaded. "People walk away two days before the wedding. My sister did it—you can too!" Others were aware of what he was like, but no one spoke up. Every family member was responsible for not intervening, as they knew I would be marrying a nightmare. They failed to warn me and they knew how bad it would be.

I told Paul about this conversation and naturally he became very angry. He actually mocked me: "You're going to become the runaway bride, aren't you?" He didn't know how much my desire to run was growing. But, my other haunting character failure, people pleasing, crushed my better instincts. I didn't want to disappoint people who were flying to Florida for a beach wedding. I ignored the red flags again, like a giddy surfer racing toward the breakers of a hurricane storm surge.

During the engagement Paul began to share stories with me of his very promiscuous lifestyle before becoming a Christian. He had been an alcoholic. I'm talking about drinking a couple bottles of vodka a night. I'm also talking about doing drugs at the same time as having orgies. My trusting self wrote it all off to God's grace. *Well, he has been saved. I don't have a past to brag about either. God has enough grace for everyone.* Paul also told me of at least two abortions (as far as he knew), and he bragged that he could have had more. He had a lot of pride in being a sexual stud and he wasn't one bit remorseful for his abortions or sleeping around.

This should have been a HUGE warning sign. He also spoke about terrorizing animals and how funny it was. This man was just plain SICK!

We went to Minneapolis to visit his only sibling. Betty and her husband were thrilled to see us. Betty and I were down in her basement when Paul wasn't there. She told me of the various ways her brother had terrorized her (and still did). She said, "I'm SO GLAD he found you. Maybe you can fix him; none of the rest of us can. I just hope he doesn't treat you the ways he has treated all of his other women." WOW! That conversation took me off guard, but again I shrugged it off. "He's a Christian now; he's better." She then said, "He loves you though. I'm sure he would never abuse you."

As we got closer to the wedding I began to see more and more red flags but ignored them. Why did I sense so much? I gave us a big engagement party. He was adamant that I pay for it. "I'll pay you back" was always his response. As we planned the wedding I put a second mortgage on my house so I could pay for it. Again, "I'll pay you back." A few weeks before our wedding he took me to meet his old girlfriend, Laura. He and Laura had co-owned a clothing store in New Jersey years ago. She was excited to meet me. She showed me pictures of their store and pictures of Paul when he modeled for their store. Then she said something that should have put me on the alert. She had tears in her eyes and said, "Paul was a monster to me. I would have given him anything and I did. He slept with whomever he could, and I paid all of the bills while he partied. One day he would be so kind and loving and the next day a monster. It seems he has found God and changed. I hope for your sake that's true." He sat there and listened to her tell me all of this. The strange thing is he wasn't even concerned with her telling me this! I guess he knew I was a woman of commitment and wouldn't change my mind.

I remember him bringing up during that time how when Joseph and Mary were engaged, it meant that they were indeed legally married in God's sight. Why didn't I question this distorted theology? I would beat myself up but I just didn't question anything.

Two weeks later friends and family began arriving for the wedding. Many had not met Paul until the night of the rehearsal dinner. He was not in a good mood before the dinner, so I was very concerned by how he would respond. As I feared, he was short tempered and cranky the whole evening. It didn't take much to put him into a rage. We had left the wedding rehearsal on our way to the rehearsal dinner. We rode in the same car to the dinner. I wanted to bring my bag with different shoes in it because I knew we may dance and I really wanted to dance with my sons. His response was, "NO! You will not bring that bag. It's ugly. It's just a bag!" He pounded his fist on the car and demanded I not bring it. My friend was standing near the car as he was yelling. "Are you OK?" he asked as he put his arm around me. "Yes. It's my fault," I said, "I know Paul hates that bag." My loved ones were deeply concerned. They left that night and cried for me.

The next day we had a beautiful beach wedding. The combination of Jewish traditions with Christian ones made it a glorious event. My boys and Paul wore beach clothes, and my great friends, the bridesmaids, looked beautiful in their beach dresses. Everyone loved it. Paul put on a great show, crying as I walked down the aisle. When we got to the reception I couldn't see very well. I realized I had forgotten to put in my contacts—isn't that interesting? I had NEVER forgotten my contacts. Literally, I think God was telling me that I had walked into this marriage BLIND!

At the reception his sister got up a made a toast to me: "Thank God Julie is a therapist. She is going to need every book and tool to know how to deal with my crazy brother." People kind of snickered but also looked at me with deep concern.

His true self surfaced en route to our honeymoon. He was in a bad mood on the way to Antiqua. For some reason he didn't like the flight attendant and treated her roughly, causing her to cry. When he made people cry, he would laugh; he thought it was funny. *How could I let myself become entangled with such a human being?* I asked myself, but I knew I had to hold it together because if he saw me cry too, he would pounce on me!

He gave the resort attendants a hard time. We went to four different bungalows, and he was never satisfied. He would yell at the attendants and actually tried to get one fired. I went to her later and apologized. She was so shaken by his behavior that she actually asked me if he was part of the Mafia. The other attendants were all very frightened of him.

I was in a crazy cycle. One minute he would scream at me for spilling a drop of coffee on the counter, and the next he would apologize, making comments like, "You'll be a good wife and won't tell anyone, right?" "You can't talk about any of this; it's all behind us." I was trapped in an abusive cycle and was absolutely TERRIFIED! I didn't know how to be safe and stay but also didn't know how to leave.

After the honeymoon, we went back home and back to work. Our relationship improved because we weren't around one another during the day. Still, I was trying my hardest not to set him off. "Don't spill coffee on the counter," he would harp. "Take your shoes off before you walk on the carpet; don't even bring a glass of water into the car; don't close doors even when you use the bathroom; don't turn on worship music." Don't, don't, don't! I felt like I could never, ever make him happy.

He told me one morning on his way to work that I had to adapt every thought and action around his thinking. I pleaded with him: "I can't do it—I just can't. I have tried, but I can't change all of my thinking around all these rules!" "You must," he said, "or we are going to have a hell of a marriage and it will all be your fault."

We decided to use my hotel rewards points for a Christmas vacation. We went to this beautiful island in Florida. But Paul the Mood Monster went with me. In the morning, if I turned on the light he didn't like, the whole day would be filled with abuse. And then I turned on the bad one. Oh, no! He went into a rage and wouldn't let it go. We rented bikes to tour the island, but he warned me it would be a terrible day because I had turned on the wrong

A Wildflower Continues Her Adventures

light. How insufferably controlling he had become. He ended up in a rage and broke my foot. He was much bigger than me and rode really fast. I kept begging him to slow down. He rode fast. I rode faster to catch up. He turned his bike sideways when he saw me coming at him fast. I crashed into him because I couldn't stop in time. He then proceeded to run over my foot with all of his weight. I screamed in pain and he took off. I was in shock and in a lot of pain as he rode off with his creepy smile. He left me alone, with no cell phone, limping on my foot for about an hour. This began a more intense cycle of abuse for the next two weeks.

So there I was: on an island, no cell phone or any way to get ahold of anyone, limping around on a bum foot. I pushed my bike around until I finally found him. Thank God it was a small island and I had some idea where I might find him. "My foot really hurts," I told him when I finally found him. "You deserved it," he said. This was my punishment for turning on the lights that morning.

That night to make it better he took me to a play in town. It was a family play so there were other families behind us having dinner as the play started. Paul is quite tall and wide. The people behind us kindly asked him to please move his chair so they could see. He blew up! He yelled, "We bought these tickets to be in front of you! I'm not budging." I was shocked. "Paul," I said, "these kids can't see through you." "You just watch me, I will push these people over the edge. I will get them to leave," he whispered. I went to the bathroom to pray I was so shook up. As I returned, the father and Paul were in a yelling fight. As predicted, the father took his family out the door and they missed the entire play. I believe that man was protecting his children from the Monster Paul.

I was scared the fear of this would intensify. We went back to the hotel, but when Paul was in an evil mood, it was just hell. Back at the hotel, I decided to lay it out for him. "Paul, you're a narcissist, a sociopath, a borderline, and addicted to sex," I told him. "You've got it," he shot back proudly. "And you're a good Christian woman and you've got me forever." That put me in a state of panic. I began a familiar refrain in my mind, a chart-topping medley in the Julie's-in-trouble hall of fame: "Maybe tomorrow will be a better day; maybe he won't do this again; I'm sure he will have a better day tomorrow." Instead, Paul's good days became less and less, and his bad days occurred more and more.

After the vacation from hell, we returned to Chicago for New Year's Eve to see my children. At that time, we were living at Paul's house, and I was slowly bringing my stuff over from my place, which was about a mile away. We left his home in Florida for the airport. I wanted to use his laptop on the plane, but he didn't want to bring it. I asked him twice, and then he blew up. "You can't use my computer!" he shouted. The worst of Paul was back. When he was in that frame of mind, he would drive fast, like 85 or 90 miles per hour, and then he'd come to a screeching stop and yell at me. I was terrified. His responses took a toll on my body and my sense of safety and stability was being undermined.

Once on the plane, he harassed and terrified the flight attendant. "This tomato juice has too much ice!" he complained loudly. He had this talent, if you want to call it that, for pushing a person until they cried. And that's what he did to the flight attendant. Then he acted very kind and concerned: "Oh sweetheart, it's OK. Everyone makes mistakes." So controlling.

We had a layover in Atlanta. While we were on the layover I was watching this couple out of the corner of my eye and basically eavesdropping as I watched the woman's partner's anger escalate. It was so intense, even in public. He was shouting, "You don't love me; you don't love me!" He made her get on her hands and knees in the airport and tell him, "I pray I can love you better." The woman looked absolutely petrified. He was treating her like a dog. "I will be a good Christian wife," she chanted to him, on her hands and knees. This scenario was so similar to my relationship with Paul, my heart hurt for her humiliation. I so wanted to reach out and hug her but knowing borderlines I knew that would make it even worse. I saw it as God putting a mirror in front of me, telling me that this was so similar to Paul.

Once we made it to Chicago, the horrible mood continued because of the weather. "It's really cold out," he said, then two minutes later, "It's so cold out." We waited for the airport shuttle to take us to our hotel, and he kept whining, so I gave him my hat and gloves and waited outside for the cab while he sat in the warm airport. As I drove to the hotel he had his zipper stuck in his shirt and he was struggling to get it unstuck. He demanded I help him. I was driving in Chicago traffic and couldn't. He started yelling at me: "You don't care about me; if you did you would stop right here and help me!"

At the hotel, Paul yelled at the check-in person, "Don't give that @#$%& the key until she tells me she loves me." Frightened, I said, "I love you." By this point, speaking those words was my way to survive. The hotel attendant knew me (I had been there many times before) and she looked at me with fear in her eyes. I knew that fear was not for her but for me.

I felt like I was in a fog, and I was terrified beyond belief. I couldn't show any emotion or pull away. I knew he was a borderline. If you pull away or detach yourself in any way you're going to be even more abused. I knew he would go into a panic and begin to control and rage even more. I walked to the hotel bar to get something to drink. Paul followed me with rage spewing out of him. He began screaming at the servers behind the counter, "You better not give her a drink till she tells me she loves me." Again, I robotically repeated, "I love you Paul."

That night, I imagined my boys meeting Paul and realizing how he had been treating me. I warned Paul, "If my boys see what you've been doing to me, they're going to kill you." Paul responded coolly: "I'm the best con man ever. No one will ever know what I am doing to you, and I know you're a good wifey and won't tell anyone."

The next day we all met. I put on a smile, but my son Matthew didn't trust Paul, and he wouldn't let Paul near his children. Paul was livid later on: "He wouldn't even let me touch their kids! They're my grandkids too!" He was truly frightening.

The following day, while my kids were with their father (Matt), Paul and I went to movie called *Big Eyes*, about a woman who's married to a crazy man who slowly gets closer and closer to killing her and her daughter. "Oh my gosh, this is my story on screen," I thought to myself. "This is happening to me. Oh Lord, what do I do?" I clearly heard him say, "GET OUT NOW!"

I couldn't let Paul know I was scared, but I knew I had to get away from him. I began making a plan with God. God continued to tell me, *I will lead you each step of the way and bring the right people around you to protect you.* Little did I know that this was EXACTLY what God did.

I would wait till we got back home to Florida. I started calling psychologists whom I knew who worked with sociopaths. I talked to others who are knowledgeable about those who are possessed demonically. I was convinced that Paul was a volatile combination of mental illness and a demonic spirit. He was disappearing for hours at a time, and when he'd return, his eyes would be spooky and scary. When he got mad, his eyes looked like they were on fire. I could feel the evil.

The day before I left I had an appointment with the brain neurologist. She would be reading my results from an MRI I had before Christmas. She was concerned that I may have a brain tumor. Paul came to the results reading with me. He acted all concerned—but it felt fake to me. Yes, I did indeed have a brain tumor, she reported to me. Yes, small, but a tumor. I felt like I had the wind taken out of me. An abusive marriage and now a tumor! HELP ME, GOD!

After the doctor appointment Paul wouldn't even let me get to the car before he started demanding we go to the lawyer IMMEDIATELY and put him on my will. "Paul," I cried out, "I was just diagnosed with a brain tumor—please let me breathe and pray through this." He was unrelenting. I told him I couldn't be with him right then and that I would be home soon. So I hopped in my car and went to the beach to pray and process with my friend Sharon. Paul kept texting me, "Where are you?! You're late!"

When I finally made it home he was livid! I told him I had spoken to my friend. "Why can't I be that person you're talking to?! I'm your husband." I didn't know what to say; no matter what I said I would be wrong. I knew after that doctor's appointment I had to get out fast. The storm was brewing.

A Wildflower Continues Her Adventures

The night before I left I had to hold everything in. He could sense me pulling away. "You're not being a good wifey. You're upset with me; I can feel it. You HAVE to put the past behind and not tell anyone. See that Christmas cactus over there?" He had a beautiful blooming cactus. "It's soft on the inside but prickly on the outside. That's you, Julie. I can snap you in a minute, so you'd better be careful."

That night he wandered the house most of the night. I slept lightly but when I woke up he was staring at me with those evil eyes. I got up to go to the bathroom, saying kindly, "I'm sorry you're not sleeping, honey." He wouldn't let me close the bathroom door. I had to leave it wide open and he continued to stare at me. I was living the movie *Sleeping with the Enemy*. I had made a big pan of lasagna and we had eaten maybe one-quarter of it for dinner. During the night he had finished off the whole thing and a half-gallon of ice cream. He learned how to devour everything in sight. He was trying to devour me.

The next morning when he went off to work I tried to be really sweet—"Goodbye, honey," I said. "I'll have dinner ready for you." I was shaking like a leaf. After he left I quickly called a couple of my friends to help me make a plan while Paul was at work.

Even though I knew I needed to get out quick, I still needed reassurance that I was doing the right thing. I knew no one could tell me what to do, that this was a hard decision I had to make on my own. My friends could hear the desperation in my voice. I was trying my best to make an unworkable marriage work.

I had not shared the details of my horror with anyone. When I called my dear friend Sharon she said, "Get out fast. He is dangerous." I quickly packed up my car, trembling. I had not been terrified like this for years (I had been a little girl terrified of my father). My heart was pounding in my chest so strongly I thought I was going to have a heart attack. I grabbed all of my belongings and went back to my house, which was only a few miles away. I called a locksmith who changed all the locks. At the same time, I called the police because I knew Paul would show up at my house soon. Within an hour, Paul showed up in a rage. The police had just arrived at my house. They told me to go back into the back bedroom and stay where he couldn't see me. I could hear him yelling but I stayed put in the back of the house. They met with him for twenty to thirty minutes, and then told me to get out of my house and go into hiding.

I packed up about three weeks' worth of clothes and left. I stayed at a hotel in the next town over that night, petrified he would track me down. As I went to the bank the next day, I found he had pulled out every penny of my checking, savings, wedding money—EVERYTHING WAS GONE! He had also canceled my car insurance. I was vulnerable in every way! I had to hock my wedding ring to pay the mortgage. But God took care of me.

The day after I left Paul, I had an appointment with one of the pastors from the church Paul and I had attended: Calvary Church. I went to the Fort Lauderdale campus to meet with Pastor Greg about running the Wildflowers program in the church. He walked in and told me that Paul had called him that morning and told him that I had left him. He said, "Julie, I need you to leave. We won't work with you unless you go back to Paul." I was shocked! "Do you know that he is abusing me?" I said as I showed him my broken foot, which had a boot on it so I could walk. I was shaking. "Please help me," I pleaded with him. He said, "Paul has been involved with our young mothers for years and is a real servant in the church." Pastor Greg acted as if he didn't believe me. "You need to leave now," he said. I asked him to escort me out of the building because I was afraid Paul would be stalking me. The secretary walked me out to my car.

A friend of mine paid for me to go to a trauma and prayer center in the mountains of North Carolina called His High Places. This was the BEST gift anyone could have ever given me. God and I did amazing work with a trauma therapist. God began to show me in very real ways my value and love. He enfolded me with so much love with the staff there and with friends who loved me over the top!

When I came home, my neighbors came over. They knocked at the door, which just put me in a state of fright. They said, "It's

OK, Julie. We have never met before, but we saw what went down a few weeks ago. We will help you in whatever way we can." She and husband were police officers. "We will be in vigilance for you. We will do anything to help you. We will help you get a restraining order." She went with me as I applied to get the restraining order. God knew I even needed someone to help me have the language to protect myself.

Paul continued to stalk me. He obviously had no respect for rules or even law enforcement. He called my job and tried to get my retirement fund, my checks. He tried to take everything from me. He even went so far as to call all major ministries I had done work with: AACC, Focus on the Family, Dr. James Dobson. He went onto my Facebook, my kids' Facebooks, LinkedIn. He took a lot of my friends and gave them his sad story. My true friends stayed; others didn't.

I continued to try to speak with the pastors of Calvary Church. I was mainly concerned, not with myself, but with the young mothers and children he was doing ministry with. They wouldn't meet with me because I had a restraining order. Basically, they kicked me out of the church so that he could stay (the same thing that the last church did to me when I left Matt).

I was searching the Bible for women who were abused. I was looking at Matthew 6—seeking help from the church and godly counsel. I had some people who wanted to meet me who had been to Calvary Church. They came to my house, a group of women and two men. They knew some of what I was going through with the church. They warned me in no uncertain terms. One of the women who came had been abused by her ex-husband, who was a volunteer leader at the church. He was beating her. She went to one of the pastors, pleading with him to help her. The pastor refused and said that her husband would stay on staff and that she needed to leave.

They also told me a story from two years prior. Another woman who was married to one of the pastors was being severely abused by her pastor husband. She too went to a few of the other pastors. Once again, they told her that she needed to obey her husband and do what he said. The sad thing is that she was so desperate for help and didn't' know where to go—she ended up taking her life. I was trembling as they told me these stories, but I thanked them for telling me the truth. Thank God for honest believers.

I had several godly men friends who were furious over how the church was handling this situation. We set up a conference call with me, Pastor Dave (who was the Boca Raton pastor where Paul attended), my friend Richard H. and Dr. Robert Rake Straw, my former seminary professor and spiritual mentor. Basically, the phone call did no good. Pastor Dave refused to listen to our cautions whatsoever. At the end of the conversation I said, "We have warned you of what this man is capable of in hurting women. This is now on you—God knows."

This was the second time this dysfunctional church scenario had happened to me. First, when I was married to Pastor Matt, his church ejected me and basically, to be blunt, told me to "shut up"! They did the same thing at Calvary. Even with godly counsel from my spiritual mentors and professor. Thank God I was strong enough to not go back as I walked away. My heart hurts for women who aren't given the support from healthy godly counsel and don't have the strength to leave. I am disgusted by church hypocrisy that doesn't protect women. I'm not saying that this is ALWAYS the case but unfortunately it is OFTEN the case.

My heart goes out to these women. I could feel God's heart bleeding for them as well. Thank God I had a good relationship with God and that I didn't take the advice to stay and be abused.

I had a great lawyer who tried to get "something back" for me financially. We went to mediation a few months later. The crazy thing is that my husband showed up strutting around in his wedding clothes! His lawyer came in and said, "What is he wearing?" I laughed hysterically (I needed that emotional release). My lawyer, the mediator, and all of us burst out laughing. The mediator said, "We will indeed be working with crazy today." Paul tried to take everything—even tried to get alimony! At the end of mediation his lawyer burst into our room and said, "Julie, I'm so glad you got away from him!" Paul lost his power that day. I felt this incredible release as he strutted away in his wedding outfit!

Although Paul took everything I had financially, he could never ever take my love for God and my dignity. We always have a choice in relationships: Will God bring about healing or will we let the prelateship cripple us? Unfortunately, Margie (whose story is above) made the choice to stay—but that was her choice. She is now very crippled. Physically, emotionally, and spiritually, she has fallen apart. God will always give us strength to do His will. But most important, he is the strongest, most reliable Husband ever! And he is also incredibly romantic!!! The greatest lover of all! He and He alone meets my every need!

Howard Marcey says, "The spiritual life cannot be made suburban. It is always frontier and we who live in it must accept and even rejoice that it remains untamed." As I work with people and God works with me, I see the greatest obstacle to realizing our dreams is the fear, even hatred of mystery. Well, that's a BIG problem because mystery is essential to adventure! Even more critical is the mere fact that God put every spiritual battle we face, every atrocity—every one of them is fought with mystery. The only way I have personally been able to hang on without going crazy with all the battles I have encountered is to realize that God is a person! Not a doctrine, not a denomination, not a building, not a list of rules. Having an intimate relationship with God is a joyful, rich part of reality as he meets my soul's thirst for adventure. Maybe part of me thought I was signing up for a comfy life, predictable, safe, and certainly not dangerous. An adventure, yes, but not a journey filled with danger, lions, and tigers around every corner, a villain lurking in the shadows to take me down.

We were born into an adventure. I know I was! I was born from an affair that was hidden, even from me. I remember as a little girl thinking, *This doesn't feel right. Why is there so much anger directed at me, when I didn't do anything wrong?* Yes, from day one and even before I was born, I was "in over my head." I remember standing in front of thousands of people to speak when I asked God, "Help me! I am in over my head here." He quickly responded, "You were BORN in over your head, love." The great thing about "being born in over your head" is that God continues to come into my fears, anxiety, trauma, and gives me COURAGE! I'm not afraid to live and I'm not afraid to die. To me, life is a wide-open adventure of love. God continues to ignite hope in this adventurous God episode. This story of life isn't about reaching the end prize; it's really the process of reaching God as the goal itself. What is God's purpose for me? For you? Whatever it may be, it really depends on Him and on his power NOW! To live the goal of having the purpose of God accomplished in me is to stay calm, faithful, and unconfused while in the middle of the turmoil of life.

His purpose is NOT the finish line but the process itself. It's simply to live with absolute certainty that everything is going to be "all right" because I see Him walking on the sea (Mark 6:49). What people call preparation is really the goal itself. God has this incredible way, really a deep knowing in the unknown, to enable and hold me as He walks with me in the shores of life right NOW! I stopped looking at the end goal, the finish line, because then I would lose the joy of every day, moment-by-moment paying attention to the precious moments in present time! Dietrich Bonhoeffer says, "To deny oneself is to be aware only of Christ . . . to see only Him who goes before and no more the road which is too hard for us." The key to perseverance when the road is rough and too hard is to keep our eyes focused on Jesus, who is cheering us on at the finish line, and right here right now, on the sidelines in REAL TIME! Is there room for God in your big adventurous life? Hang on! It's a big beautiful ride!

Your Time

- I wrote about my own nightmare. What is your nightmare?
- How do you handle your nightmare? How would you have handled this? What would you have done if you were living my nightmare? Sally's nightmare? The woman in the airport? Margie's?

- If the women (and I) were in front of you, what would you have said to them? How could you have helped them get out of their nightmares?
- What would you have wanted the man in front of you to say? What if he didn't follow through?

CHAPTER 18

A Miracle Unfolds

Another Brain Surgery, Another Miracle!

IN DECEMBER 2014, WHEN they found my brain tumor, I felt like I had been hit with a bat. Kind of like you have a foreign object inside of your head that is unwanted, almost your enemy. Waiting for it to grow or praying it doesn't grow, if you get side effects, you start to see the world differently. Every time you have a slight pain in your head, it's easy to think the worst! What if it's growing? When you see someone who has had a stroke or is maybe paralyzed, you think the worst. What if that's me? Will I be paralyzed in my face? Deformed?

I was overwhelmed because less than a month later, I left my ex-husband. I had to concentrate on keeping myself safe—I had to put ALL my energy into leaving and protecting myself. I had no fight in me left to even think about the real fact that I had a brain tumor GROWING in my head. But I knew I had to follow the doctor's orders in every way, so when she told me to come back in six months for a follow-up MRI, I kept my appointment.

Even though I knew there was a possibility that the tumor in my brain had grown, it was basically a "remote" possibility somewhere in the back of my mind. I never really had time or energy to "pull it up" and consider what that meant. Honestly, I had learned to fragment my mind. I was holding pain or thoughts of tragedy

A Miracle Unfolds

in the basement of my brain, the cellar of pain that I didn't want to "dig up." I was in spiritual mode—and gosh darn it!—I was going to get through this divorce as whole as I could be and then let God help restore my broken heart, broken body, and broken life. So when I got the results back that my tumor had grown, I literally felt like I had been thrown under the bus in every way!

The neurologist said, "I have bad news," when she gave me the results. "Your tumor has grown—a small yet progressive growth." Yes, I heard *small*, but more than small, I heard *progressively growing*. As I look back on that day the doctor gave me my results, I felt more scared and alone than in all my years of a truly different life. (Although honestly, I'm rather stunned when people say I've had a difficult life—how could it be difficult with all the joy and love I have received?).

But yes, this news was frightening. God had taught me to go to Him first and that he would give me peace. I left the doctor's office and couldn't wait to get to the car. "God—help me!" I pleaded. The doctor had told me to come back in three months for another MRI, so I made a few phone calls to friends, gave my tumor to God, and went on with my life.

In November 2015, I had a follow-up MRI. I remember crawling into the machine, scared yet experiencing God's peace. In a few days my doctor asked me to come in for the results. When the doctor had me come in and would not give me results over the phone, I knew it wouldn't be good. And it wasn't. My tumor had "significantly grown." My doctor suggested that instead of removing it, we do a followup MRI in three months or until I had side effects. I left the office again feeling scared, lonely, and conflicted.

Why would Dr. G. wait to do something with this tumor unit I had side effects? It didn't feel right.

I called a few good friends and my doctor son Mathew. They too thought it was odd to wait for a tumor to grow and have side effects. They told me to get a second opinion. I didn't know where to go for this second opinion.

I felt like I was playing Russian roulette with my brain. I called a number of brain surgeons and decided I would go to the first doctor who called me back. Dr. Rishi Sheth's assistant called me. I made an appointment. Imagine my shock when I walked into my appointment and Dr. Sheth knew me! He had been in the operating room in Long Island when I had my traumatic brain injury surgery!

I knew right then that was a divine appointment and that I would be safe in this surgeon's hands. To help me feel better I put my doctor son Mathew on the phone. He confirmed with Mathew that I needed to have surgery soon and not to wait until there were side effects. We scheduled the surgery for right after Christmas, January 2016. The three-week wait was rather scary. Although I had MRIs and other tests regarding the tumor, they wouldn't know if it was cancerous until they removed the tumor and did a pathology report.

Again, I was in a time of my life where ALL I had was my faith. The choice of God and his love became so thick and profound—it is all I had. I had been down this path before, desperately clinging to God. The journey of faith and trust was becoming very familiar to me. Dr. Dan Allender says, "Redemption touches us more deeply then tragedy. . . . But without tragedy there could be no redemption." I began to pray in this scary "bend in my road" that I would learn to suffer well. That I would find true hope, and that as God shattered my dreams, He would create in me an appetite for better dreams, dreams that are from my Father. My Heavenly Father, who has always faithfully taken care of this daughter. In an incredible way I have found my deepest worship in my tears.

I choose joy over fear.

Dr. Sheth told me in my pre-op appointment that I would have a scar across my forehead that would probably last a good year or more, but that he would be doing plastic surgery.

When Dr. Sheth was taking me into surgery, I remember asking him, "Doctor, have you ever done brain tumor surgery on someone with no side effects?"

"No, Julie, I can't say I have, but you are going to do great and we are doing surgery to prevent side effects." In praise to God, I fell asleep.

I woke up with my daughter Bonnie Joy and son JonMichael at the foot of my bed. I felt no pain, just a cloud of joy—I was

A Miracle Unfolds

on cloud nine with God. They were waiting to hear the pathology report. The report came back clear—NO CANCER. As much as I could muster up the energy, I cheered! They cheered—the room was a holy explosion of JOY!

They left a few days later after making sure I was all settled at home. When they left I began to write of all the joy inside of me! My recovery bed became a sanctuary of healing love.

Here is one of my writings:

Greater Possibilities of Love

But I am like an olive tree flourishing in the house of God; I trust in God's unfailing love for ever and ever (Psalm 52:8).

Let yourself be drawn into greater possibilities of more love. The wonder of hidden dreams and desires await. Redemption, transformation, and restoration will become fully known as the Father, King, and Romancer pours more of the Kingdom of God within you, giving you an eternal prescription for a life well lived with the divine intimate presence.

This intimate presence is so rich and profound within me that I sometimes blush as my God expresses his tender romantic love to me. He instructs me with renewed passion and direction for the rest of this adventure of life. I am speechless in the beauty and wonder I see.

We have been given the gift of the suffering Christ who awaits and welcomes us Home. His divine Spirit gives language to the risen Christ of Hope and Joy awaiting within us. As He builds his house in our heart, He draws and beckons us to more love. Let us burst forth with profound gratefulness.

My bed became a sanctuary of healing joy.

My bed became a sanctuary of healing joy . . .

This brain surgery was truly a "miracle in disguise." I was told by my brain surgeon, Dr. Rishi Sheath, that I would be in bed at least three to four months. After only three weeks I got a call from Dr. James Dobson's assistant Brian. Dr. Dobson had read *A Wildflower Grows in Brooklyn* and was requesting I come to Colorado Spring to do a radio interview. "Well," I responded. I was told I need to stay in bed for three to four months and it's too soon. But I will ask my Great Brain Surgeon what he thinks."

"Okay," Great Brain Surgeon responded.

In the meantime my kids had to leave to go back home to Chicago. After they left one rainy Florida night, I thought I better drive to the store and pick up a few groceries. Dr. Sheath didn't say I couldn't drive! (Of course I probably didn't really ask him!) So I got in my car with my still fragile body and some confusion. The store was only about five miles and I could do this! I was a little overly confident. About a mile away from home I got confused and went over a curb—a BIG curb. As I got out of the car I was surprised as I walked around the car—all 4 tires were totally flat! Oh my! I was in a state of shock and knew I couldn't wait until a tow truck came to get me and the car. So . . . I drove home on four flat tires. As the tow truck driver arrived at my home, he said in shock, and also with a little smirk on his face: "I have been a tow truck driver for over 20 years. Ma'am, I have never had a car that has four flat tires and four destroyed rims. Congratulations!"

Thank God I had good insurance!

So when it came to going to the doctor, word had spread among my friends that I really shouldn't be driving. Darn! So my friend came to pick me up to have my first post-op appointment. My friend Ginger bought me a beautiful orchid. I was thrilled to have her bring this beautiful plant! Thank you so much, Ginger! But I want you to know I don't really do well with plants, especially in hot Florida. I promised I would take very good care of this orchid. So off we went to the doctor.

I told Dr. Sheath about my offer to fly to Colorado Springs and do a radio interview. I really wanted to go! "Well, Julie, I have never told a patient this but you are ready to go! You are doing great!"

As I prepared to go to the interview with Dr. Dobson, I was a little vain about the LARGE scar/incision that was all across my forehead. I'm talking about a thirteen-inch ugly scar. I had a large gauze pad over it and was always wearing hats. I felt it was SO UGLY! I told a friend about my scar. He immediately put me on a National Prayer call. After the call I went into the bathroom and closed my eyes as I took off the bandage. WHOA! My scar had disappeared! I had no scar. I was on my way to Colorado to interview! YAHOO! No Scar!

Well, I had such an incredible connection with Dr. Dobson. Actually, we were going to have one interview but we had three. The staff gave Dr. Dobson and me a STANDING OVATION. Dr. Dobson said His staff had NEVER done that. Those became the number one interviews, voted on by the listening audience!

When I arrived home I was in awe at all of what God had done. I had another appointment with Dr. Sheath. When I got home from Colorado, I walked in and Dr. Sheath said, "WOW!!! Julie, what happened to your scar! It's gone! I have never had a patient that has had such miraculous healing and NO SCAR! I wasn't even seeing a remnant of it."

He pulled in another doctor and his nurse. He said "I'm a good surgeon—right? They said, "YES! You're a great doctor." He said, "Well I want you all to know I DIDN'T Do this. Only God could do this miracle in Ms. Woodley." I watched Dr. Sheath's eyes sparkle. God had used me to ignite this very successful surgeon's faith.

I left the office on a spiritual high. Dr. Sheath had also done more extensive tests on the tumor for any sign of cancer. NO CANCER. NO SCAR. TOTAL HEALING!!! WOW!!! Alleluia!

I went home and began to dream and plan for what God and I would dream and desire for the future. IT was only about a month after my friend Ginger had given me the lily. I was leading a conference call one day. Someone else was talking as I was looking at this beautiful lily. I was thinking, *WOW!* I can even keep a plant alive—God is indeed working in me in every way. As I looked closer at the plant a thought struck me! This plant isn't really! It hasn't dropped a leaf—it's not a bit brown. I was right—the lily was plastic! I burst out laughing on a very serious phone call. I was laughing hysterically. The people on the other end heard my "plastic plant" report and joined me in contagious laughter. God is SO GOOD! And so funny!

Chapter 19

Fixing My Eyes on Jesus

Fixing my eyes on Jesus

I CONFESS I LOVE reading the ancient paths of dead people. To me they really aren't dead; their words and examples are alive and well in me. I will soon meet them in heaven—it's going to be a grand reunion! As I study their lives I see that they have faithfully followed a tried and true road that led to an abundant life, lives bursting with what matters most, a life everlasting. We too can live that path by listening to the hope that whispers to us and beckons us every moment of every day. "But joyful are those who have the God of Israel as their helper, whose hope is in the Lord their God" (Psalm 146:5). My passion as I move forward on this adventure is to give my all and finish well. As I pray and bring comfort to those I dearly love who are getting closer to heaven, I see a joy in the depths of their eyes. There is a sparkle because they know they are "going home" to their heavenly Father. All of their hope is in Jesus. They are learning to "suffer well" in the middle of the battle. Their eyes are fixed on Jesus. Of all people in my life my friend Sharon has taught me the essential lessons of Christianity. To love when I'm scared, to give when it's not fair. She has taught me to be a feminine warrior. As I think about what I want said at my eulogy, I desire to have the courage to stand up for those in need, to fight for the weak ones. To live a life of wholehearted integrity.

I desire to live a vibrant life that others are drawn to because of the joy, love, and mercy that God has planted inside of me. This longing for the romance of God beckons me to not harden my heart because someone hurt me. To not lose heart when the assaults feel fierce. To not deny the wounds and awful tragedies of life, but to keep my heart alive and beating with love in the face of trauma, tragedy, and pain. To live like I'm loved in the face of assault. For me to lose hope would have the same effect on my heart as to stop breathing.

I love to study the life of Jeremiah: He lived roughly 2,600 years ago. A wide-eyed prophet who was living through violent and tumultuous times, he wrote:

Go stand at the crossroads and look around
 Ask for directions to the old road,
The tried-and-true road. Ask where the good way is, and walk in it.
  You will discover rest and what is right for your soul.

Those who went home before us knew that dying is returning home. A passage to new life. I pray I can live this next chapter in my big beautiful story well so I may become more prepared for the final passage. Jesus so very kindly takes away the sting of death as he leads us to the place where the deepest desires of our heart will be satisfied!

So today and to the end of my days, I will hang on to the truth that Christianity is exclusively original. It alone offers us God's saving hope. IT IS THE REAL THING. Jeremiah knew it! The ancient prophets and disciples knew it, and most importantly, Jesus knew it! I resolve to be single-minded in following Jesus all the day long. On my knees now, bowing with my heart, body, and soul lined up in a poster of prayer,

I pray,

God, I am blessed to know I can trust your original plan of redemption! Fixing my eyes on Jesus, the author and perfecter of faith. I'm living God's love song! That's what I'm talking about!

Sharon, the love of my life.

You, Sharon, are the love of my life. When others saw a wild spirit, you saw beauty. When others saw too much passion for God, you saw my heart beating with the wild love of Christ. When others saw extravagance that made them uncomfortable, you embraced and loved my extravagant heart for God, which was exploding, sometimes in very extraordinary bold ways. You have taught me the most important lesson that we as Christians need to learn, to live loved. You taught me to be a mother when I didn't have a clue; you taught me how to love well, even when I walked away from toxic relationships. You taught me who I am: a woman passionately in love with God, my children, my grandchildren, and literally all of humanity. You, my love, so filled me with love that I couldn't help myself but to invite others, many others, to join us in heaven. You are now teaching us all how to "suffer well" as you joyfully run into heaven ahead of us. And as you said the other day, "Invite many into heaven, Julie, my sweetheart, so they can join us in eternity." Your big blue eyes are so filled with love it takes my breath away. You have been my sister, my dearest friend, my intimate ally, my home. I and my children long to serve you in whatever ways we can here on earth. And then sweetheart, oh the party we will have in heaven! As Corrie Ten-Boom so eloquently stated, "When I enter that beautiful city and the saved all around me appear, I pray someone will say to me, it was you who invited me here"

CHAPTER 20

Why Do I Do This?

I HAVE BEEN ASKED this, and at times, asked myself and God. Why not comfort, God? Why not a plush life?

I write, I dream, and I go into others' (and my own) horrific trauma with my Savior and listen . . .

I listen to my Savior's thoughts and heart in another's pain and atrocities because I have been born to do this!

I was not born to step away, run away, or become numb to evil, suffering, and injustices. I was created to run towards the traumatized, those who have been sexually exploited or trafficked, the slaves of today.

I experience this hard work of a trauma therapist because I KNOW! I know heaven comes down. My prayer is that I can run into hell and usher in heaven. I know because I have lived and experienced hell on earth. But more than that—HEAVEN came down. Christ came down and met me, held my heart, cried with me....my heart beats with His.

What does heaven do? Heaven leaves heaven. It's a place of comfort, plenty, purity.

My question is: Where are you, Church? Are you in the dungeon, the filth, darkness, and suffering?

Acts 17:6 says: "Those men have turned the world upside down."

Has the Church gone into the dungeon so the dungeon becomes the Church? I know that God has entered into the dungeon of my heart and transformed my heart into a heart that looks like

HIS. God in His power became little and became one of us so I may be HIS.

I have come to know there is no me; there is no them. There is only US. When God's people worship and separate themselves untouched, they are not worshipping the God of the Scripture. There is nothing in the Scriptures to suggest that being complacent, neutral, and deaf is Godly.

Sadly, I see that the body of Christ has failed to see trauma as a place of service. "It's too messy!" I have heard this many times. And they are right! It is messy! We may get bloody shirts, snot in our hair from the many tears, and often a broken heart. But isn't that where Christ enters in?

Our first call is not to a place, be that churches or dungeons but to a person of Jesus Christ.

When we love and obey Christ, no matter what the cost, we must first bring Christ into our own dungeons—we know them and so does Christ. We cannot hide our dungeons, whether they be pride, pornography, or self-hatred. We and He know our dungeons.

But most importantly, we know that God interfaces with this world as it is. He leaves the higher and descends to the lowest. He leaves beauty and enters into chaos. He leaves pure and enters filthy.

So back to the original questions. I am called to the work of the dungeon. The work that my Savior has graciously given me.

Because God carries my anguish, I know it and I bear witness to it myself as I enter into unspeakable atrocities.

I too live the push-pull between the need to speak and the need to hush. . . . I know the tension exists because it resides in me. At times the ROAR of the Lion within me is so very strong—the ROAR of trauma. But greater still I know the song of HOPE. It is music to my ears and heart.

I know that my broken "happily ever afters" are over because I KNOW my Savior will hold my heart. He will hold my dungeon atrocities and love me in the sick mess! I HAVE LOVED. This is all I have to offer a hurting world. And ya know what? It IS ENOUGH! Because it is the work of our Savior . . .

Epilogue

A Wildflower Moves to Chicago

In June of 2016 (4 months after brain surgery) as my children had requested I packed up my house to move to Chicago. Not an easy task packing up a house after brain surgery. But God put an unstoppable mission on my heart to be near my children. And my Great friend (more like a Sister, part of my heart for 37 years).

I remember one night as I was packing up the closet where all of the ministry materials were. It was about 3 am. I had been working for over 8 hours in the closet. I worked so hard packing up boxes I had boxed myself in. Hungry, thirsty, weary beyond belief I was boxed in-literally. I didn't even have the strength to dig my way out so I fell asleep boxed in. That's one thing you experience after brain surgery is utter exhaustion where you can't move another muscle. I guess the fact that I had had not just 1 but 2 brain surgeries had a little bit to do with it. I woke up with a very sore body at around 6 am. I had been curled up in a ball like a little Kitty.

I cried out to God—what in the world am I doing! He said to me "you didn't ask me for help! You just went ahead and did it-you need others help-just ask. So I called my Son Jon Michael—"Honey, will you come help me, I physically can't do this?" Yes, Momma, of course. He said and we made plans to fly out from Chicago to help me.

One of the reasons I moved to Chicago is that I was working with Timberline Knolls as their Ministry outreach representative. They were looking forward to having me move close to them so I could take on a position as one of their Christian Therapists. As

Epilogue

soon as I got to Chicago they had me come into a meeting. I was excited to take on some hours as a Therapist. I was totally shocked when instead of offering me hours they ill mated my position. They said I didn't do anything wrong they just no longer needed me to fill that position and didn't have anything else for me.

I went into a bit of a panic. What am I going to do? God will I sink financially? I desperately clung to God. In the next 2 years he kept his promises. It hasn't been easy—-I filled for bankruptcy for myself personally. Not only did I lose my job but I also had around $27,c00 to pay for out of pocket medical expenses. The ministry struggled big time as well, I was in the beginning stages of creating a video curriculum (much like the Wildflowers program) for women and men that had been sexually exploited called "Shattered and Restored." Our ministry had raised $23,100 to create the film. Right before I had brain surgery the man who was going to create it took all of it. He said in order to produce the program we were to send him a retainer of all of the money we had raised. Well, trusting me overnighted him the money. Bottom line he took it and we received NOTHING except heartache. So I also submitted all of the credit card debt the ministry had accrued into bankruptcy.

So for the next few years I learned how to live on little. It didn't seem to matter that for a few weeks all I had was a powered diet someone had bought for me years ago….I had such a thankful heart that overshadowed every bit of poverty! God has made me so very rich how could I not be SO GRATEFUL for even powdered food! I began to live the verses about financial trouble: "The young lions lack and suffer hunger; But those who seek the Lord shall not lack any good thing." Psalm 34:10

"The Lord is my shepherd" Psalm 23:1

God has provided me each and every step of the way. I have led many to Christ and been that prayer person in the disability office! I have bowed for many as I waited for my next brain scan. God provided food stamps and Medicaid for me! I must admit I am an overflowing fountain of gratitude! I have a BEAUTIFUL life!

So now I live in Chicago spending time with my children and my greatest friend Sharon in the whole world! I now am working as a trauma therapist with the specialty of sexual trauma all over the country and beyond! I have the great opportunity to work those with complex sexual trauma—Priests, women that have had their homes broken into, victims of war trauma, rape, sexual exploitation . . . I am truly blessed to use my gifts to bring healing to many who have suffered trauma. I have firsthand understood Suffering and the heart of God.

I have had many people die in the last few years. I wrote this right after I found out my cousin Dean was murdered by his wife:

My eyes are leaking today. So much loss, so many good-byes. So much death. I know that they are "going to a better place" and that I should be rejoicing that they are going home. But today, I just leak. I weep and find comfort in God holding me and crying with me. I let myself leak today. I have "leaked" for many of my clients in their losses (often alone). I have held many while they "let go" but today, I can't hold my cup of sorrow any longer, it is overflowing. I leak... I'm sitting on my porch on this beautiful Saturday night. A bright red cardinal has also appeared to sing to me as I lament. "God, we are all so human down here! Such a mess. Addicted, afraid to live, afraid to feel all of the emotions of this beautiful life. Pain, joy, love, hate, loss, grief, ecstasy. We blame everyone else! The government, our parents, teachers, the medical system. We grasp, we cling, and we are desperate." "Desperate for what, my Love?" You ask. "Desperate to be loved, my Lord." You say, "I'm here, Love. Tell them I love them! Tell them to feel! Love, joy, pain, sorrow. It's all part of the plan. This big, beautiful adventure of life! All they need to do is say YES!!! I have so much abundant life in store!!! Open up your hearts and be ready. You will live loved. No fear in love. Be ready to live loved!" Your wild lover, God.

Bibliography

Curtis, Brent and John Eldredge. *The Sacred Romance: Drawing Closer to the Heart of God*. Nashville: Thomas Nelson, 1997.

Eldredge, John. *Walking with God*. Nashville: Thomas Nelson, 2008.

Kidd, Sue Monk. *When the Heart Waits*. New York: HarperCollins, 1990.

Langberg, Diane. "We move into the journey of their hearts." *In the Wildflowers Counseling Series, Step 2*. By Julie Woodley. Minneapolis: Honest to God Media, 2008. DVD.

Langberg, Diane, Jason Li, and Paul Singh. "They release their shame." *In the Wildflowers Counseling Series, Step 3*. By Julie Woodley. Minneapolis: Honest to God Media, 2008. DVD.

Nouwen, Henri. *Turn My Mourning into Dancing*. Nashville: Thomas Nelson, 2004.

Wright, H. Norman, Matt Woodley, and Julie Woodley. *Surviving the Storms of Life: Finding Hope and Healing When Life Goes Wrong*. Grand Rapids, MI: Revell, 2008.

About the Author

JULIE WOODLEY HAS PROVIDED Christian counseling for 27 years. Julie provides educational outreach and training about women and trauma to churches, ministries and Christian colleges around the country. She has also recently written 3 video productions.

She produced the DVD series "In the Wildflowers," which trains professionals and others how to help those who have suffered from childhood sexual abuse heal. She also produced a DVD series for the trauma, healing after suffering from the pain of abortion, "Into My Arms." She also recently completed a production called "Cultivating Ecstatic Joy, Even In the Midst of Life's Tragedies."

A speaker, author, film producer and trauma expert, Julie holds an M.A. in counseling and a certificate in theological studies from Bethel Seminary. She is also an Ordained, Licensed Minister.

She holds a certificate in Sexual trauma healing from the National Center for Crisis Management in collaboration with the American Academy of experts in traumatic stress. Her website is www.JulieWoodley.com or www.Restoringtheheartministries.com

www.ingramcontent.com/pod-product-compliance
Lightning Source LLC
Chambersburg PA
CBHW070915150426
43193CB00011B/1468